Answering HIS Call

HOW TO SERVE GOD AND COMMUNITY WITH LONG-TERM MISSIONARY WORK

AMANDA DYER

First published by Ultimate World Publishing 2025
Copyright © 2025 Amanda Dyer

ISBN

Paperback: 978-1-923425-29-3
Ebook: 978-1-923425-30-9

Amanda Dyer has asserted her rights under the Copyright, Designs and Patents Act 1988 to be identified as the author of this work. The information in this book is based on the author's experiences and opinions. The publisher specifically disclaims responsibility for any adverse consequences which may result from use of the information contained herein. Permission to use information has been sought by the author. Any breaches will be rectified in further editions of the book.

All rights reserved. No part of this publication may be reproduced, stored in or introduced into a retrieval system, or transmitted in any form, or by any means (electronic, mechanical, photocopying, recording or otherwise) without the prior written permission of the author. Any person who does any unauthorised act in relation to this publication may be liable to criminal prosecution and civil claims for damages. Enquiries should be made through the publisher.

Cover design: Ultimate World Publishing
Layout and typesetting: Ultimate World Publishing
Cover Image Copyright: BCFC-Shutterstock.com
Editor: Marinda Wilkinson

Ultimate World Publishing
Diamond Creek,
Victoria Australia 3089
www.writeabook.com.au

TESTIMONIALS

The path to missions is very challenging. It's full of difficult questions, an overwhelming number of obstacles and a reliance on God and his leading.

Amanda has walked that journey having spent 8 years serving in Central Asia and Eastern Europe with her husband Geoff and their son Will. They faced setbacks and challenges leading them to change organisations and countries but through that built a wealth of experience and knowledge that is invaluable. Amanda is passionate about using that experience to help others navigate their own path to cross-cultural mission.

Over the past 2 years I've walked the journey to mission with Amanda as she mentored, supported, encouraged and prayed with me through to the final stages of my application and in building team support.

Amanda is a generous mentor providing wise, practical and relevant counsel. From her own experience she understands the questions, doubts and fears that I have had and talked and prayed through those with me. Practically, she has helped me develop and execute strategies to build team support and communicate well with my supporters. The encouragement and advice she has provided has been invaluable in my journey.

Kelly, with Interserve Australia

My wife and I had the privilege to serve alongside Amanda and Geoff in Central Asia. Amanda is kind and dedicated. She has a heart to always minister with excellence, and for mentoring, and is committed to walking alongside the people God gives her.

Reinert, now serving in Norway

We were holding a team meeting, planning a service, and sharing. At the end, Amanda came up and said, 'I think you need to talk to one of the girls, something has happened to her.' I was so busy with the service then that I did not notice any of this, although she was my disciple. Even now, I sometimes remember Amanda and this situation, and I teach myself to be more sensitive. And I always pray that I have people like Amanda on my team who are focused on others and their wellbeing.

I am immensely happy that Amanda has written this book, because she is a wonderful person who loves God and has many stories from which we can learn.

Zhadra, serving in Uzbekistan

Amanda is a woman who is open, hospitable and always puts God first.
Dinara, serving in Kazakhstan

Amanda, you care for people a lot; I know that's true because there was a time when you stood up for me in my struggles. You are a great listener and are always fully invested in the things you are doing, and in the people you are with.
Janis, serving in Latvia

DEDICATION

This book is dedicated to all those would-be missionaries that might use this book to help them answer the call on their lives to serve overseas and bring much glory to God.

CONTENTS

Testimonials	iii
Dedication	vii
Introduction	1
STEP 1: Calling	5
STEP 2: Positioning	21
STEP 3: Fearful	35
STEP 4: Agencies	49
STEP 5: Praying	63
STEP 6: Moulding	77
STEP 7: Fundraising	91
STEP 8: Yielding	105
STEP 9: Resting	119
STEP 10: FAQ	129
Afterword	141
About the Author	145
References	147
Explanation of the Symbols	151
Acknowledgements	157
Contact Amanda	159
FREE WORKBOOK available online	161

INTRODUCTION

How beautiful on the mountains are the feet of those who bring good news, who proclaim peace, who bring good tidings, who proclaim salvation, who say to Zion 'Your God reigns!'

Isaiah 52:7 NIV

While this book is about becoming a long-term missionary, it also relates to the call on all of us to be part of the great commission. It doesn't matter where you are in your walk with Jesus, you can be part of the bigger picture. Serving is an important part of the body of Christ.

This book is designed to encourage and excite Christians to step up to the commitment of becoming a missionary. I have included parts of my personal spiritual journey, alongside some tips on dos and don'ts. The sequence of the steps that I have written follow the process of how I believe most people progress from the initial calling to getting on the plane. I have also included examples of missionaries who have worked in different locations, in different fields and with different skills. I have not used current missionaries because I do not want to draw attention to them.

I have written for those looking for mystery and adventure. To those who have received a hint from God, a nudge or a moment of inspiration. We work together, discovering things like where you might serve, how you know God is calling you and how to choose an agency to work with.

Working with many missionaries over the years, the thing that most concerned me was the lack of preparation they received before coming onto the field. That was my inspiration for writing the book. If I help people ask the right questions and be informed before they leave home, I will be happy.

I have specifically not written an academic book. I didn't want it to be filled with biblical references and theology. I wanted the book to flow and be easy to read, allowing the reader to explore their own journey with Jesus. We are all unique and Jesus communicates with us in His own way.

The book does not contain all aspects of becoming a missionary. What it does contain is nine steps that can each be applied whenever you are ready to receive that information. There are practical action plans and suggestions of things that you might try as spiritual disciplines. Routines that are good to get into.

I have always admired those who have a relationship with Jesus. The easy-going way they chat about being

Introduction

with Him, His sense of humour, and the simple way Jesus has of teaching us how to live life. We often complicate relationships. Overthinking if something has a hidden meaning or if someone has a hidden agenda. When we take Jesus at face value, we learn His message is all about love. He loves us unconditionally which is something we find hard to comprehend. Much of the New Testament is written by people in the language of their time. It's not all about laws or instructions but letters and stories of people's experiences. Just normal people like you and me. Our stories are unique, and Jesus encourages us to share our stories as testimonies to Him. I have tried to follow their example by using everyday language. Remembering how it felt at each of the different steps with its challenges, joys and disappointments.

Jesus sends out ordinary people in every generation to the four corners of the earth, to save the lost, to care for the poor and to heal the sick. Is He sending you? Get in touch with Him and find out. You're never too old, never too young. It's not about being perfect, it is so much more about being available. Lord, send me.

STEP 1

CALLING

We walked along the riverbank and fed the ducks. We chatted easily about our children and our spouses who had passed away 2 years previously. I liked this man, but he had so many questions. It's like I'm in an interview for a job I've not yet applied for. I think to myself maybe next week I'll bring along a picnic lunch. *Oh, so you think there's a next week, do you?* my subconscious asks. Our shared conversation is about the difficulties we are having being on our own and we talk about dreams and desires for the future. He says, 'I have always wanted to be a missionary.' I responded, 'So what are you doing about it?' At the time I didn't think my answer was significant, but it was a challenge. Like the sound of an engine on a steam train, it put in motion a series of events that led to 10 years of our lives together as missionaries.

Today, more than ever, people are looking for purpose. We are looking for direction. Whether we are believers or not, we are asking the question, what is it all about? Where do I belong? How do I fit or where do I fit in? As we grow older the questions become intense. What is the reason I am here? Being believers we have the advantage. We know why we are here: we are all called into mission to share the gospel and make disciples. God who called us prepares our lives for His plans and purpose. As believers we sometimes ask the question, what can I do to be of service to God? Every generation of Christians asks the same questions. We all possess different gifts, but we all can serve. The reason for discovering our calling is because there are so many jobs to do inside and outside the church.

Missionary work is a calling from God. The purpose of being a missionary is to share the gospel, make disciples, care for the orphans and the lost, and be a voice for the vulnerable. Some of us are called into ministry full time or part time and some of us are not. There are people called into the government to work or the private sector, education, medical or social justice, many different spheres of influence. We can't just be called to one area, the church. We need to be called into all the areas of the world to make a difference. The need for missions is global. Our world view must be wide and our tolerance high as we step into our calling. No one mission is more important than any other mission – it's all important to God.

There are some people who, towards the end of their lives, do not feel fulfilled. They do not feel the peace of God in their hearts and minds. They may have served in all sorts of different areas including the church, but they are dissatisfied with their lives. Unfortunately, they're frustrated, disappointed and even angry. They have regrets of lost opportunities or roads not travelled. God's purpose has eluded them. They have not found their calling; they may have served in various aspects of God's kingdom, but it has not worked out the way they thought it would. Their expectations have not been met.

Discovering your calling early in life is quite significant to how you feel when you get to the end of your life. We can all do good things, but that is not the same as God's plan for you.

Paul says in the scripture, 'For when I preach the gospel, I cannot boast, since I am compelled to preach. Woe to me if I do not preach the gospel!' (1 Cor 9:16 NIV). Apostle Paul knows there are real world consequences if he refuses to carry out his calling. I have met many Christians who have told me they were called to be missionaries in their youth, but they did not do anything about it and now they are older they wish they had followed His calling. God invites us to participate in a relationship with Him. He always asks us to take little steps to come closer to Him. This relationship works two ways. We learn to trust God; He learns to trust us. Just like in a marriage or a business, this relationship is built on trust. If broken, it is difficult to repair. God forgives us but sometimes we don't forgive Him.

The obedience of serving God through His word and by His spirit is a privilege and an honour. It comes with an exciting adventure, and we are never quite sure where the road is going to take us, but the mystery is part of the journey. We may start in one direction until God moves us in another direction in His timing. We never know what is before us until God reveals it to us and the part we are to play. Seeing God work through us is exhilarating. Watching how He brings all the pieces together, the fruit of our labour is miraculous. I often sit in awe of how He makes it all happen. To fulfil your calling and find your purpose in life is more than rewarding: it's a transformational experience.

Reverend John Flynn (1880–1951) founded the Australian Inland Mission (AIM) as well as the Royal Flying Doctor Service. AIM served the remote central and northern regions for almost 40 years to minister to the spiritual, social and medical needs of people in the outback. A young airman Lieutenant Clifford Peel who was also a medical student inspired Flynn through a letter to create the Flying Doctor Service.[1]

Calling

In this chapter we will hear people's experiences of the calling on their lives to serve God in missions. We'll explore what future missions might look like and whether there is still a place for long-term missionaries.

Local missions

Serving locally works for many people as not everyone wants to go abroad to answer their calling. There are always opportunities in our own backyard. When a church is built with a heart for missions, it grows people with a passion for missions, allowing the Holy Spirit to work through it. When a church is outwardly focused it is thriving. To achieve this we use local programs that are actively engaging in sharing Jesus' teachings such as prison ministry, or Alpha and others. It is hard to believe, but there are people currently in Australia who haven't heard of Jesus. We need to find holistic ways to work with other churches to share the gospel.

In the past we had crusades where all the churches worked together to save souls. Traditionally, local missionary work was based on sharing Jesus while partnering with communities to meet a need. It may be a one-time event repairing a garden in a school or continuous support like providing a soup kitchen. Recently I have discovered missionaries are being sent to Australia to share the gospel. This was a surprise to me. There are times when missionaries are paid to work here in Australia, such as Bible translators who mostly work in indigenous communities. This may be something people explore as a career path.

Short-term mission

I often wonder what short-term missions will look like in the future. The industry is changing. Churches are being run like a business – bums on seats! That may sound a little harsh but there seems to be money-raising programs for buildings more than salvation. The trend today is for short-term missions to join a project with a specific job, a maximum timeframe, set costs and measurable outcomes. There is also a thought within the church that young adults should experience a brief overseas trip/adventure as a rite of passage.

This is not only true in Australia, but Geoff and I were part of this type of experience in Kazakhstan. We helped take a group of Kazakh youth to Finland for a short-term mission trip. As they prepared to leave their country, we watched their faith grow as they learned about God. We witnessed with them God's miracles as they had no money and no way of raising funds, but God is faithful and in came the funds they needed. We watched God heal them from physical and emotional pain and suffering. These young people had never known what it was like to be in a country with religious freedom. Three of them were baptised in the sea in public, something they could only have ever dreamed about, as Kazakhstan is not only Muslim, it is also a landlocked country. This was a very valuable experience for those young people, one they will remember throughout their lives. This may be also true for the young adults in Australia going out on a mission trip, as it is possibly their only opportunity to leave the country and see God at work.

Unfortunately, short-term missions can sometimes be culturally insensitive. If done badly it can be very detrimental to the economy and community being served. Foreigners working in areas traditionally served by the locals or where locals are expecting money like Santa Claus coming to bring gifts is not helpful. In the future it is hoped we develop a closer relationship with those in the global village, particularly with so many different cultures living in Australia supporting and caring for their brothers and sisters in foreign lands. We can improve communication with foreign local communities throughout the year, not just during a short-term mission trip. There is a place for short-term missions.

SHORT-TERM MISSIONS
BY KAREN EVANS
(KARDINIA MISSIONS LEADER)

In recent years short-term missions (STMs) have encountered their fair share of criticism. Are they beneficial? Do they cause harm? Are they a waste of money? What role do they play in the wider mission picture?

Done well and with the right motivations, preparation and understanding I believe STMs are hugely beneficial and important to both the individual participants and the receiving organisation. In fact, I believe God can and does work through STMs to move people closer to Jesus and build His Kingdom.

Here's why:

- Empowered partnerships: STMs established in the context of partnership between the sending church and receiving organisation strengthens the relationship. It's a long-term commitment. The primary purpose is for the discipleship and cross-cultural experience of participants AND the provision of activities that best serve the receiving organisation, and the Kingdom work they have been called to do.

- Cultural exposure develops a global perspective: STMs expose participants to different cultures and cross-cultural work. The experience of new foods, customs, languages and ways of doing creates greater understanding of how God is at work in the world. Spending time with local people and long-term missionaries helps participants to see a global church in action and may inspire a life filled with sharing the gospel.

- Building relationships with Christians around the world: STMs often involve visiting churches, organisations and communities where participants can connect with local believers and national workers. Meeting people from diverse backgrounds can be a profound experience, creating a lasting connection and a deeper understanding of how our brothers and sisters live, work and worship around the world.

- Personal growth and transformation: Participants often go on a STM with the belief they will make a difference to the communities they visit but I would suggest a STM tests and challenges the individual. Exposure to a different way of life challenges preconceived notions, living in the uncomfortable brings a new perspective to their faith journey and may even motivate a life of service either on the field or at home.

I've seen people return from a STM with renewed hope in humanity, challenged to make a difference in their world and sphere of influence and people determined to 'live differently' because of their experiences. Their passion for the receiving organisation manifests in storytelling, testimony, prayer, connection to long-term missionaries and national staff along with provision of financial resources. God is at work in their lives just as He is at work in the local and global context.

I've seen receiving organisations, long-term missionaries, national staff and communities encouraged to press on with the work they have been called to do with a renewed understanding that the sending organisation is united with them in mission. Partnership for the long haul is valuable for the provision of connection, prayer support and financial resources but also in receiving teams that bring a variety of skills and abilities that equip and empower the local work.

With more than 15 years' experience in STMs, I've learned many lessons about preparing and leading teams. I am always encouraged and inspired to keep going when I see the transformation in the lives of the individuals who have been on a STM team. Seeking to understand, recognising that differences between cultures aren't good or bad, they are just different and having a posture to learn are just some of the things I encourage for first-time STM participants.

I am convinced more than ever that STMs are an important part of both the local church and mission landscape, and we should not underestimate their power to make a lasting and profound impact.

Traditional long-term missionaries

Those who went to foreign lands sharing the gospel for a lifetime taught children, and built schools, hospitals and churches. In the current climate, we are often supporting missionaries for projects such as building houses, teaching technology and engaging in social justice reform, which doesn't always mean sharing the gospel. Part of the job of a long-term missionary may be to do these things alongside hosting short-term mission trips, but this should not be their primary focus. These activities need to be the vehicle used to share the Word.

We need to remember missionaries are still part of the church family. Unlike our experience, when we were sent out from our church, and were removed from the membership register and only thought of at mission time, most long-term missionaries go with an agency who provide many of the basic supports needed. But there is still an important role for the sending church. Arrangements need to be made to send out support people to visit missionaries while on the field. It can be a very lonely time for them arriving in a new country, especially single people, so a visit from your home church is greatly appreciated. Currently, many missionaries are returning home after only 12 months because of homesickness or disunity with fellow missionaries, so clearly something is not working. Missionaries need more than just being prayed for and then sent on their way and sometimes being asked for video clips for a church service. There needs to be more thought in forming a two-way relationship.

There is a change in the dynamics of the church. Pastors are often torn between sending missionaries abroad when the need is so great at home. Long-term missions now average 5 years, and their financial support is often tied to performance. Missionaries are required to be accountable, with measured outcomes, set length of time, allocated funds, specific projects and tangible numbers of people helped. Less about God, more about man's accountability. Within Christian circles, there are competing ways to serve God, just like in the Australian sports industry. People have lots of choice which sport to play, people have lots of choice where and how to serve God. Long-term missions are out of favour, it's not encouraged by many churches because it is expensive and hard to measure the value of the impact on the community they are serving in. There are also many different charity organisations to give our tithes and offerings, so why give it to missionaries? Many people want to support locals of a specific country directly. The belief is that the money would be better spent going straight to the country for those in need instead of supporting someone on the field. Missions are a complex business with no easy answers. We can't make any hard and fast decisions about ruling something in or out based on current trends.

Is there still a place for long-term missionaries? I believe there is. But we may need to redefine missionary. We need to look at how we fund missionaries or how they can fund themselves. We need long-term missionaries to break new ground. To be embedded in communities where we cannot simply get access by sending a short-term mission trip. It is far more dangerous than being in a country that accepts Christianity. This type of work has no accountability, no measurable results, only the guidance of the Holy Spirit. It's about living and working with unreached people groups, prayer walks, learning from the people, sharing the hope of Christ in a hopeless situation, teaching the people the love of Jesus. This is not for the faint-hearted. The risks are high, the challenges are great and there may be little reward.

Calling

GEOFF'S CALLING

For most of my Christian Walk I supported missions work in some way. I had my own business and was able to give substantially to missions and to specific missionaries. And that was great to do, to be part of what others were doing.

Then my eldest son Tristan did a couple of mission trips, to Timor and India. My daughter Joanne also volunteered for 6 months in Peru. And my second son Lachlan went to PNG to do missionary training with his church. I supported him and was praying for him. But I was feeling jealous. Now jealousy is a sin, so I was repenting of that but still feeling jealous. As I prayed more, I came to realise my jealousy was from God. He was calling me to missions also. Somehow, God was wanting me to be a missionary.

As part of my exploring mission organisations, I connected with a group called Second Wind. They were promoting missions by encouraging those a bit older, over 50, with 'So your mortgage is paid off, your kids have left home or are self-sufficient, what then are you doing with the rest of your life? Could this be a season where you could be involved with missionary work?' This resonated well with me, but I didn't really know what to do next. I did talk to other missionary groups and got on their mailing list to learn more.

Meanwhile, Amanda and I met, a couple of years after our spouses had died. We agreed to talk but no deep relationship. Early on I shared with her my heart for missions. Instead of saying, 'that's very nice' she responded, 'So what are you doing about it?' That shocked me a bit and I think I replied, 'I'm waiting for God.' We have since met many who have been 'waiting for God' but missed the calling they felt on their lives. Amanda then encouraged me to do some studies to prepare myself for that, not at all realising she was determining her own destiny to be a missionary with me. I took up a master's degree at the Bible College where Amanda was doing her theology degree, and the rest is history ... or His story! We were soon dating and then married and fulfilling God's purposes and missionary calling as partners and a team. Which is still happening in somewhat similar but different ways ... but that's another story.

Questions

What if I am so confused by all the feelings I have that I don't know how to move forward?

This is a common feeling. These are big decisions. But choosing to do nothing and waiting for God to do something may not work. There are times to wait on God and there are times to do something. Now's the time to do something. Voicing our ideas and praying about them but then leaving it with God is a good way to see how the Holy Spirit will lead.

Calling

What if I have tried to get an answer from God in the past but nothing happens?

God is working very hard to communicate with you. Look at all the different ways He has shown you love in the past. He loves unconditionally. He forgives all we have done simply by repenting. Lay your heart open to receive His forgiveness. This will open a door.

What if I lose sight of the path I'm on?

Take a step back, or two or three steps. Taking time out to meditate, go on a retreat or just stopping to rest is invaluable. One of the remarkable things discovered from Covid stories is how much people needed to rest, take stock and reset. Thankfully we don't need another Covid to rest and reset.

Action Plan

Pray for specifics. Ask God direct questions. Expect a direct answer. It may not be the answer we are looking for. It may be something unexpected. Allow your imagination to take hold of the seed for a time.

Test the idea with God's Word. Even if it seems impossible in the present, continue to pray. God will reveal more to you in due course.

STEP 2

POSITIONING

So, you're called to be a missionary ... what are you going to do about it?

When we place ourselves in God's hands, He will love us unconditionally. He will guide us gently and lovingly into a place where we can serve Him. Positioning allows God to move us forward in a direction He is moving. If we stagnate, or if we are undecided or lukewarm about what we are doing, He can't work with us. In scripture we read, 'So, because you are lukewarm – neither hot nor cold – I will spit you out of my mouth.' (Rev 3:16 NIV). Jesus uses this statement to describe the church at Laodicea. It's frustrating when people are not one thing or another, just apathetic.

Alternatively, there's a passionate verse in Isaiah 6:8 NIV: 'Then I heard the voice of the Lord, saying, "Whom shall I send, and who will go for us?" And I said, "Here I am. Lord, Send me!"' We don't just get sent. There is a process of personal transformation which is only possible through Jesus. Personal transformation starts with grace and forgiveness and purifying our hearts, taking away our sins and shame. The transformation doesn't happen overnight, but it does happen.

Confirming our call to be a missionary is often a daunting feeling. The first way to know God has called you is through scripture. Scripture teaches us, encourages us, corrects us in His ways. Secondly, confirm that you will follow Him fully and willingly, including all the costs associated with the commitment. Acknowledging the presence and power of the Lord your God and King.

Developing our servant heart within our local community helps build a stronger sense of purpose within our inner self, as we learn to adjust to the changing needs of the community in which we live. All the people who are serving God in full-time ministry have a developed relationship with Him. While we are all called to serve, some are called to serve full time. Those people are placing everything

Positioning

they have in God's hands to serve Him. They work on their relationship with God daily. Learning to be moulded and yield to His will daily is part of the process. This is a good reason for positioning ourselves and getting a better understanding of our calling. Getting to know who we are in Christ and how God can use us.

Finding 'my tribe' is commonplace these days. We live in the world, but we need not be defined by the world. Our identity is defined by the community we associate with. The reason we want to find our tribe is because we need to gain strength from others around us to point us to Jesus. People who love the same stuff we do. We need to gain ideas and share our concerns with others. It's important not to be an island, not to cut ourselves off by putting everyone at arm's length only to work on our own. It's easy to do. Finding a significant, like-minded group of people who have a heart for missions helps us decide firmly on a course of action.

As our transformation takes place it especially affects our power to act. As we begin to possibly move in a different direction from our friends and families, we may struggle. We may find ourselves being placed where there is advantage over others. It may become isolating. We may feel more vulnerable to attacks by the enemy. The closer we come to God the more the attacks will take place. God may position us in a place for strategic purposes. Be aware it is easy to lose motivation or lose sight of the end goal. These are the other reasons for positioning ourselves in the right places. As He purifies our heart, we want to be with the people who understand those changes that are

Answering HIS Call

happening to us, help us when we are low, lost or lonely and share in our wins and all the revelations we receive.

I would like to think all churches are centred around sharing the gospel with the lost, but in today's Christian world there are many different flavours. Some emphasise different aspects of Christianity and they don't all put a lot of emphasis on missionaries. Long-term missionaries are currently out of favour in many churches. Some churches are only focused on their local community and still other churches are opting for mission trips within our own country. I believe there is a place for all sorts of mission work including long-term overseas missions.

From Five Barley Loaves tells the story of five women, seemingly insignificant for the challenge of mission, who began a global movement to send out Australian Baptist missionaries. Their work began in Bengal in 1885 where they were few among many, hence the title of the book. After hearing a sermon, the five women embraced long-term years of service in India, Asia, Africa, Central America, Eastern Europe and the Middle East, as well as with our own first nations people.[2]

Positioning

What is expected of a missionary?

In some ways the expectations of a missionary are unchanged. There is still the great commission which remains unchanged. In the 21st century there is a drive towards social justice issues through helping others within a charity framework, by spreading God's love through making use of a missionary's skills, talent and training. In the past missionaries have achieved many great things such as building hospitals, schools and churches but these types of projects are fewer these days because of the complex nature of the countries missionaries live in and the lack of supporting funding to complete these structures.

Today, the main purpose of a missionary is to be part of a community by living and working in that community. To be part of a community is often to be working among the people, eating what they eat, dressing in similar clothes, living in the same type of housing and walking instead of driving in some cases. Being fully immersed in a community and sharing God's love despite your circumstances is a challenge to say the least, but people see Jesus in action. There is much criticism of the way missionaries live on the field. They drive nice cars, live in upmarket housing and eat western food. They are separate from the community they are hoping to serve. There needs to be a balance between living and serving in a community and adapting from our culture into theirs. The criteria for being a missionary is not all the same. There are many ways to the mission field. This story is not the usual way to the field, but it shows us how important it is to follow God's lead even if you don't know where it is going all the time.

THE DOCTOR AND THE PILOT

Janis and Danny lived on the outskirts of a city in Australia. Janis was a nurse's aide, and Danny was a cook at the local café. They had two young children and lived in a rented house. They loved Jesus and had gone to church all their lives. Life wasn't going very well but they never complained. One day at work Janis saw a notice that offered a scholarship for students to help them become doctors. She liked the idea of being a doctor, she liked to help people. Together they prayed. Janis decided she would apply and see if it were possible. To her amazement she was offered a scholarship.

She asked Jesus to help with every step because this was a whole new learning curve and language which she could barely understand, and she was afraid she was not good enough to be a doctor. Not long after Janis began to study, her father passed away and her mother came to live with them. Janis' mother did a lot around the house which helped them all. Janis worked and studied very hard. At one exam she felt the Lord's hand over hers as she tried to write. She knew she was in God's will. A couple of years into her degree Janis' husband lost his job. He was devastated as you can imagine. Danny and Janis turned to God as they always did, and they felt God tell them Danny was to become a pilot. Danny had a little money from a pay out at work and Janis' mother had a little savings. Together this enabled him to get a pilot's license.

He became a crop duster for the local farming community and life seemed to be going well. Until Janis' mother became ill with cancer and passed away. Janis was not able to save her mother even though she had all this training to become a doctor. This was a low point in her journey with Jesus. She didn't understand why God would do this. Her faith took a beating. She graduated as a doctor despite her disappointments because she knew that would have made her mother proud. The following year she worked as a doctor and began to emotionally heal. At the end of the year their youngest child graduated from high school and went off to study at university. As Danny and Janis did every day, they prayed. They felt God call them to become missionaries. The Lord led them to an overseas mission agency, and they teamed up with a flying medical clinic that serviced a huge area in the depths of Africa. They did not go through the usual channels to become missionaries, but they were faithful, committed Christians who our Father God could work with.

How to gather information and learn the jargon

I personally found gathering information and learning the jargon was difficult. So much of it was overwhelming. Geoff had been involved with missions a long time but for me it was a whole new language. Sometimes I just used the strategy from an old saying 'fake it till you make it' as I navigated my way around the different mission-minded folk we were mixing with. Some language is universal but other terms are specific to the agency you are with. Some of the missionary terms you might encounter are:[3]

- Global church – body of believers around the world
- Sending church – home church who supports and prays for their missionaries to undertake mission work overseas
- Receiving church – receives mission workers to assist them with the ministry they are already doing
- Missionary kid (MK) or TCK third – culture kid who are growing up overseas with a mission family
- Home assignment, furloughs or sabbaticals – taken as rest time either at home or abroad
- Host country – where a missionary is living and working
- Globalisation – where local churches take the lead in reaching their own culture
- Mobilisation – a group who connects with people who are interested in becoming missionaries
- Member care – a group who offer a range of services to missionaries as they deal with all sorts of issues on and off the field
- Intercultural ministry – a group of people who have the same world view or are native to one culture or community and serve and minister to others within that same culture

Positioning

- Polycentric sending – the mobilisation of global workers into missions from all over the world.

And the list goes on and on … I put systems in place so I could access the information instead of carrying it around in my head. I sometimes felt force-fed. Every area of work has its own language or jargon and it's a matter of just talking the talk until you understand it. Engineers talk their own language just like lawyers and doctors, and missionaries are no different. If we study missions at university or via an online course it helps broaden our knowledge, language and worldview. It doesn't need to be very formal: just finding a few missionary subjects and doing them is useful. It's not necessary to do a whole degree, unless the agency you have chosen requires a degree, but that's explored in the next step. Bible colleges offer some interesting short courses to get you started in learning the history, culture and language of mission work. Knowing the history helps you understand how things are done or were done and why. Moving in this direction also helps you to start talking to like-minded people who can help guide you, influence you and instruct you with their wisdom.

It's also important to develop your own wisdom and discernment. Take your time to digest all the information coming to you, but once you feel like you are in control find a driver. This is a highly motivated person to move you in the direction you want to go. Some people have loads of energy and are intensely passionate about missions. These people are good to be around. They get things done – get on their wave and journey with them. You'll be amazed at what you can learn and achieve.

A warning about facts and their meanings

There are times in our journey with Jesus we think that an event or incident is Jesus telling us something or taking us in a particular direction through circumstance. Be aware of the meanings you attach to what appears to be factual. Most of us do this without even realising we have done it. For example, a person may tell you they lost their parents in a car accident therefore there cannot be a God. The accident was a fact, but the meaning was something they had attached to it. Someone else may say they were able to rent an amazing house down by the sea, therefore, there must be a God. The two things are mutually exclusive. We can attach any meaning to any event. Which is why the Bible tells us to test everything. 'Do not treat prophecies with contempt but test them and hold onto what is good, reject every kind of evil.' (1 Th 5:20-22 NIV)

Our emotions can make us very vulnerable at times, especially when we are trying to discern the direction our lives are going. We don't want to sabotage ourselves with negative messaging. It is natural to attach meaning to events and incidents, but it is possible not to attach meaning to an event. It is simply something that happened and we are emotionally very happy or very sad about the facts. But the facts don't mean we deserve what happened, good or bad. This story was an event. It set in motion a series of other events which we attributed to God's favour. But was it?

Positioning

DINNER AT JOE'S BROTHER'S HOUSE

Geoff and I were invited to dinner by a couple from our church. We didn't really know them, so this was a good opportunity to get to know them better. Geoff chatted with the host telling him he was an engineer. 'Oh, Joe, my brother is an engineer,' he said. 'Where does he work?' asked Geoff. 'He works in Kazakhstan,' said the host. 'That's interesting, we are planning to be missionaries in Kazakhstan. Who does he work for?' Geoff replied. 'He works for Shep & Co.,' said our host. 'But that's who I work for!' exclaimed Geoff.

The following morning Geoff went into the office to find this person he had never heard of. It turned out Joe had a desk not too far from Geoff's, but since he was never there, they had not met. Some weeks later Joe arrived at his desk. Geoff introduced himself and chatted about Kazakhstan. 'We have just won a contract in Kazakhstan and the first part of the project is being done here,' said Joe. Geoff was surprised and interested to know what the project was all about. 'Do you want to be involved in the project?' Joe asked.

Geoff was amazed at how these circumstances were unfolding. Later, a few Kazakh engineers visited the office. Geoff chatted with them about work opportunities in Kazakhstan and discovered the company had an office there. Geoff never did engineer work in Kazakhstan, but we valued Joe's friendship while we were living in Central Asia.

31

Questions

What if I can't meet the expectations of being a missionary?

As we learned, it's other people's expectations, not God's. God uses all sorts of people for his mission field, and we all have disabilities seen and unseen that make us think we are inadequate and not up to the task. But if we keep our eyes focused firmly on Jesus, we will meet His expectations.

What if I tried learning the jargon and gathered information and I am none the wiser about deciding to become a missionary?

There is the possibility that God wants to direct you on a different path for now so you can gather different skills in preparation to get on the field. Sometimes God's steps do not seem logical to us but if we are obedient, eventually we will begin to see the wisdom in His steps.

What if I misread the sign God is sending me?

We all struggle with this question and none of us get it right all the time. Test the water, try different things. Discernment takes practice. Just remember God is trying as hard as you. Keep trying, persistence is the key ingredient to walking with the Lord. Eventually you will feel confident seeing His hand on your life.

Action Plan

Find a 'tribe' to belong that has a mission focus.

'Memory verse' is a discipline we often learned as a child. In fact, it is a useful tool to have as a missionary. We sometimes find ourselves without our Bible or our phones and to have verses at the ready in times of healing or comforting others is handy.

When on missions, we need to remember we are not the hero, or an answer to their problems, but we are sharing in the learning. The relationship needs to be in the context of a two-way relationship. We are often unprepared for the sights that we are seeing. Sometimes in our rush to help we do a job the local people can do for themselves. This is not helpful.

STEP 3

FEARFUL

What are the benefits of overcoming fear? The reason we need to overcome our fears is to enable us to grow into who we really are no matter what we choose to do in life. Nothing happens if we don't make it happen. Unless we make changes to our lives and try new things, everything will remain the same. If we think about it, there's comfort in everything being the same. We wear the same clothes we know look good, we drive the same car feeling safe in it, we stay in the same house as it is familiar, we stay in the same job because it is secure. What happens when one of those stable components changes? How do you deal with changing fashion, the loss of a car, a house or a job? There is no guarantee these things will remain the same. Dealing with fear allows you to take advantage of whatever life throws at you and whatever opportunities God gives you.

Whenever you are about to move forward and take new ground there will be people trying to oppose you or discourage you. It says in scripture, 'I will stay on at Ephesus until Pentecost, because a great door for effective work has opened to me, and there are many who oppose me. When Timothy comes, see to it that he has nothing to fear while he is with you, for he is carrying on work of the Lord, just as I am' (1 Cor 16:8-11 NIV)

Feeling fearful has physical symptoms such as feeling sick, headaches, mental fatigue, anxiety, feeling overwhelmed, out of control or sensing impending doom. These are all symptoms of fear. Worriers as they are known become stressed about everything from the weather to world devastation, but worry doesn't fix anything. It only gives us high blood pressure and cancer. While fear is our natural protection mechanism against danger, it's important to get the balance right between maintaining control of fear and allowing fear to inform us. Facing your fears can be liberating and transforming.

Feelings of emptiness that cannot be fulfilled with what we are doing, or everything we try, doesn't feel satisfying. We may ask, what else is there? What is the meaning of life or what is my purpose? To answer these questions, we need to stop trying to be perfect or worrying about what others think. Are we going to find our purpose if we worry about it? If we stress about being incomplete or empty, is fear helping with that? This is your journey; there are no right and wrong answers. It isn't a one size fits all approach here. No-one can write your life story. 'Just do it' as a famous footwear brand would say.

Some people feel stressed once they decide on a direction. What comes next? The great unknown. Scary huh? If it challenges you, that's a good thing. You really want to explore it but you're afraid because you may not be successful. You might be afraid of taking responsibility for your actions. Many times, money is the reason people give for not taking the next step. Dreams and ideas of things we like to do don't start with money. Some people share their adventures, or we read about what exciting things other people are doing and wonder, how come other people do interesting things? Why can't I do something exciting too? Why do they have so much energy to do stuff? It seems so easy for them. The scripture says, 'All this I have spoken while still with you. But the advocate, the Holy Spirit, whom the Father will send in my name, will teach you all things and will remind you of everything I have said to you. Peace, I leave with you; my peace I give you. I do not give to you as the world gives. Do not let your hearts be troubled and do not be afraid.' (John 14:25-27 NIV).

There is an emphasis in our culture to conform. We want to look the same as our friends. We want to hang out with the same group to have a feeling of belonging. To find our tribe. We believe if we do not conform, we will become isolated, alone, rejected, abandoned. This type of conforming can lead to loss of self-esteem and depression. Peer pressure, bullying, all those things that make us feel lonely. Becoming an individual and finding inner strength within our group may be the answer. Or, trying a new group which allows for fresh ideas, creativity, new relationships, growth and development.

If we don't overcome our fears, we become stuck and stale and uninteresting to be with. We sometimes may feel numb or bored with life. Never sharing new ideas or things we have learnt. This is a kind of a victim mentality. Everybody else has got a better job or better life or a better spouse or better parents or better friends or better everything else than me. That's a victim mentality. The negative messaging we send ourselves is destructive. Woe is me. That small voice inside your head that will not find the courage to step out and be seen. Have you been cast as the ugly duckling when in fact you really are a swan?

In a 2022 article by Jen DuBos, the Stenzel Clinical Services suggest that fear of the unknown is universal. We have no control over the future, we don't know if we'll get sick or be able to get away from danger or our hearts will get broken. Along with the universal fear of the unknown they have identified that the most common areas of fear fall into three categories: death, abandonment and failure. They go on to say that as we live longer and more secular lives, and become more isolated through technology and individuation, our fears increase. But this need not be the case, because our core beliefs have a weighty influence on whether you'll be ruled by fear or rule over fear.

Fear is a natural emotion that arises in us when we sense danger. The fear of the unknown is something we all fear. Being afraid to step out of your comfort zone does not allow you to explore your inner self. Parts of your personality, character, skills and ability lay waiting to be discovered.

Patricia Wilkinson (1944–2011) was a shy Australian medical doctor who became a prominent campaigner for the ordination of women in the Anglican Church. She also had a heart for missions in Africa and served for SIM in Jos, Niger and then in Galmi, Niger at the surgical and obstetric hospital. She met and married Robert Brennan in 1971 and moved to Nigeria where she worked as a physician with SIM and he taught mathematics. They returned to Australia in 1973 where she continued to support SIM[4].

Managing the fear of the unknown

Am I hearing God correctly? This was my first question when I thought about being a missionary. When it became clear this was the direction my husband and I were heading, I thought, 'What do I know about being a missionary?' I was fearful of what came next and what was unknown. There were so many things to learn, and I did not feel equipped to deal with all the changes. I was trying to juggle many new things at once. A new husband who had a lot more energy than me. Four stepchildren who were grieving the loss of their mother and didn't want any changes in their lives. Our relationship had happened too quickly for our children. When we married, we left all our children in their own homes except the youngest and rented a house quite a distance away, in a different neighbourhood from the houses we owned. We went to different churches, so we had to find a new church that worked for all of us. I was trying to finish my theological degree, and Geoff was working and studying too. It was messy and it was stressful. We had a big adventure in front of us and it was exciting and challenging, but it was only by God's grace we achieved our goal. I took a deep breath and began to write down all the things that needed to be done and organised, then sorted them in different categories. We prayed and asked God to just give me a little bit to do at a time because I could only see the mountain.

Overcoming objections

There is a cost involved in this work – it may be loss of income, loss of career prospects, loss of relationship. I asked myself, was I cut out for this type of lifestyle? Others may ask you similar questions. Why would you want to be a missionary? Have you outgrown your current job? Are you looking for a change or challenge? Why would this type of work satisfy you? Are you escaping your current situations?

Fearful

Many missionaries are back home in 5 years after taking an average of 3 years to be trained and equipped to go. Is it worth facing all the anxiety and fear to be a missionary? There are many personal challenges we must overcome in the process long before we arrive on the field. After initially getting our head around the idea of becoming a missionary, we begin to share our heart's desire with others. It's difficult to deal with other people's objections and there is a possibility of a negative reaction. It may not be easy.

I understand if you feel afraid, because it challenges families. They will not want you to leave. Depending on your circumstances you will be taking away their grandchildren or you'll be leaving your children, or you'll be leaving your parents and friends. There will be all sorts of reasons why families will object. The family structure is the fabric of our society and wanting to veer in a different direction other than what is the norm, will be met with disappointment. We are often afraid when sharing with our families and friends because they will have all sorts of questions and concerns. Like your age. Are you too young or too old? Should you be married or if you're married should you have children before you go? Is giving birth in a foreign country safe? They may worry if you're single you won't find a spouse!

Being prepared helps with resistance and objections. If you know the questions people are going to ask, and have the answers prepared, it will give you confidence. Eventually most people come around, they adjust. Their fears are because they love you and want what they think is best for you. Learn to be resilient, be assured that it's what God wants. He provides strength and a way of dealing with obstacles. Many fears come under the category of rejection – not fitting in, being alone, not being liked or being abandoned. For those who struggle with low self-esteem, shame, guilt or lack of confidence, acknowledging your fears will help you overcome them. Knowing most people are also afraid of rejection helps too. Remember you are worthy of doing what God has in store for you. Making sure you are taking care of your emotional needs is super important.

LEAVING OUR CHILDREN

Geoff and I have six children from our two previous marriages. When we felt called to be missionaries, we agonised over the timing of this commitment. When we married, most of our friends and family assumed we would move into one house or the other or sell both and move our children who were all still living at home at the time into a big house like the Brady Bunch. In the beginning we thought we would take our youngest son Will out of school for a gap year and explore the different types of work being offered in different countries and return to a place we liked once our son had finished school. But it soon became obvious God had His own plan. We accepted a contract to serve in Central Asia for 2 years. This meant leaving behind our five children and taking the youngest. Geoff was anxious about sharing this news with his youngest son for some time. Will visited his aunt shortly after he got the news. He was devastated. The bottom had fallen out of his world. 'Let's see what the school you are going to looks like,' said his aunty. The kids in the video clip didn't wear uniforms. Will thought that was fantastic and was excited to go. We worked with each child to encourage them in the direction they wanted to pursue. We prayed for them and pleaded with God to help them find their place in life. What we saw was God placed a family around each of them. Each of them had the security of a place where they felt loved and cared for. We felt anxious leaving our children at this time, but God is faithful. They did far better in His hands than ours.

Worry doesn't work

We are often afraid of things God has already thought of and has planned well in advance. Before we are confronted by a situation, we feel anxious about it. Even though I know in my heart that God has got it all in hand I still have moments of being stressed out. It seems I have a natural ability to worry, like most mums. There are some people, it seems, that can say 'yes' to everything, expecting to work out the details later. For most of us it takes time to build up to this level of confidence. Some decisions require more thought and processing than others. For some, the fear of failure comes from perfectionism. However, it is possible to step into any new challenges without fear. It may be called a leap of faith, or stepping into a situation without knowing what we have let ourselves in for. We often worry we will make mistakes and feel we won't be successful. If we do nothing, then nothing will change. If we listen to that inner voice that says you can't do something or you are not good enough, you'll fail every time. Then you become stuck on that treadmill of always failing. Don't worry!

DRIVING IN ALMATY

Having arrived in our new country we discovered everything was a challenge. A different culture meant learning a new way of life. We lived out of town, so a car was essential. We bought a cheap second-hand car, a Toyota RAV4. Like many cities in the world, driving is a challenge. Unmade roads, few road rules ... and then there is survival on the road. My husband drove us around and I was happy just to be a passenger. Unfortunately, shortly after we got the car my husband lost his license, so we walked. It became clear to me that I was going to have to drive, the weather was becoming colder, and we had outreaches to do. The car was a manual and I hadn't driven a manual in many years, but with a bit of practice I managed. I began by driving down the dirt roads to the local shop to buy a few bits and pieces. Then I extended my driving range to include the neighbourhood. I asked a German friend of mine how she drove in the city. She said, 'I never look in the rear-view mirror and I pray.' I applied the same principle. I just focused on where I was going.

Over time as I got accustomed to the traffic conditions, I began to feel more confident and could look around but initially I was afraid of everything, other cars putting us at risk, damaging the car and even getting lost. Most of all being stopped by the police who would want money for some made-up reason. I started taking small risks to drive locally then bigger risks because the reward was worth the risk.

God never asks us to do anything we haven't been prepared for. I had learned to drive before being a missionary. I had overcome difficulties in the past relating to driving so I knew I could overcome this fear by taking small steps. If we analyse it, the process is simple. We take small steps until we are ready to take the next small step and so on. This is how we overcome every fearful challenge. Never look too far ahead because that will only make the task daunting. You will be overwhelmed by what's in front of you. We are learning all the time, and it feels good using our gifts and abilities.

Questions

What if I am afraid to take a leap of faith?

God never asks us to do anything other than in our own time. There are so many different types of missionary experiences out there it is quite possible you may find a position that is like your current type of work. The timing of when you go is different for everyone. It may be years before He is ready to send you.

What if I do not go?

Missionaries often do the training and don't go onto the field. There are many different reasons for this. We lose sight of the end goal, are attacked by the enemy, choose a different path. All sorts of reasons, none of them are right or wrong. Just keep seeking God in all you do, and he'll have a path for you.

What if I'm not sure if I'm called to be a missionary?

The idea of becoming a missionary was in my head long before it was in my heart. But what did my heart say? The heart is where God connects with me. It's the best indicator I have of knowing what God is saying to me. God will confirm your calling in different ways. He may arrange confirmation through a friend or circumstances or events to show you that 'yes' this is what He is asking you to do. Allow Him to confirm it to you.

Action Plan

Shout out loud, 'I am a missionary' just to know what it sounds like, to get used to the idea.

Write down your fears and share them with God. Journaling helps us overcome our anxieties. It is a spiritual discipline that has many benefits. A good thing to practise.

Tell your family how long you are away as this will give them hope. A timeframe is something people can comprehend and knowing you will not be gone forever helps.

STEP 4
AGENCIES

An agency is your most important support network when you are a missionary. They have many tools and resources. They arrange documentation, support staff, housing, transport, guidance, local knowledge and language learning. They provide all manner of invaluable information.

I observed in my time in Central Asia that there were several different reasons why people left the field. Sometimes they came unprepared, sometimes they could not do what they came to do. They were anxious, frightened and didn't feel secure, leading to fears, tension and heartbreak. Many times, the agency was the reason why people left the field. The agency did not prepare them well before they came or had not prepared a place for them on arrival. At times I saw people in conflict with their agency partners, a personality conflict which meant they were unable to continue working with the group they were with. Some agencies can be unbending, without flexibility. Unable to make changes, they do things in a particular way. At times that creates hurt and disappointment. Although missionaries are mostly adaptable, it's not always easy to see God in the picture. We read in Proverbs 3:6. NIV: 'In all your ways submit to him, and he will make your paths straight.' I sometimes felt that our path was anything but straight. Not only ours, but the path of others as well, as I share in these stories.

I remember an Australian family who were sent into the countryside after 4 months of language learning in the city. They hated being in a small village, but the agency would not allow them to relocate back to the city. They subsequently left that agency and joined another.

Another family I remember arrived from Brazil. Ana and Lucas had spent a year in England learning English with two very small children, and we met them at the border. They didn't have visas for the children, their agency had only provided visas for the parents, so they were only allowed to bring the children into the country for 100 days on a parent visa. We took them home because their agency was not there to greet them. Both parents and children were panicking and stressed. They were told they had to leave and go back to their own country to secure the right visa that included their children, which they didn't want to do. They knew that would mean having to raise more money to return. They were afraid they might lose their opportunity to come back. This was a devastating time for them, they had spent so much energy trying to get onto the field. It looked as though they may not start their mission work. In the end they went to a neighbouring country that accepted them, and gave them visas for the whole family. Having made the error, the agency did work very hard to find a suitable solution.

I've seen another family with nine children on the field that only lasted a year. They went home very despondent and heartbroken because there was a lack of support on the field for that family and they didn't feel very well taken care of by their agency. Both sides have expectations that need to be met so communication and honesty is vital.

I've also met with a family on the field who served for more than 10 years, then without warning their church (not an agency) cut their funding. In the beginning the church had insisted that they didn't get support from anybody else, that they were solely connected to this one church and now this church was pulling the plug, so that was hard for them. If they had an agency who could have advocated for them, they might have stayed.

I've also seen families leave for schooling. The children get to a certain age, and they leave the country because the school system is inadequate. An agency usually researches schooling before you go.

I know two people who wanted to marry who were with different agencies, but one of the agencies insisted they reapply for their position, effectively removing them from the program. Because they would not have qualified a second time, this prevented them from marrying.

The list goes on with heartbreaking stories of failure and rejection. The reverse is also true. I have seen many happy people who have told me stories about their experiences with their agencies where they know they wouldn't have made it through without the support of their agency. So, it's important to find an agency that fits with your personality, your vision, your goals, your strengths, your weaknesses and the level of control you want them to have in your life. They need to get you! Really understand you. Also, you need to work collaboratively with them. This is a two-way process.

Alan Tippett (1911–1988) was a Methodist minister and missionary. Tippet's missiological research for various mission agencies took him to Mexico, the Solomon Islands, Polynesia and Ethiopia. He then moved to the USA and wrote many books encompassing theology, anthropology, missiology and history.[5]

Agencies are our business partners

You need to be able to trust the agency, that they have your best interests at heart. You need to know the agency you have chosen will not let you down. They all have different styles, criteria, training, experience and expectations. They provide for you a service and support to make your journey easier. This is a long-term relationship, so you need to get it right. A missionary agency is an organisation that supports people who want to serve God full time, usually in a country other than the one you live in. It is possible however to be a missionary in your own country and there are agencies who will help place you in locations where you can serve.

The agency is not a church, but they are often associated with a church. There are several agencies that have no affiliation with a church and accept people from different denominations. An agency has structure. They will have a board, a mission statement and a set of guidelines which have been formulated from their beliefs and values. They have criteria for being associated with them along with expectations to be fulfilled. They offer different levels of control, support and benefits. Some require you to raise support, while others pay a salary.

Where in the world do you want to serve?

This is an important question that you need to ask when you are discerning or trying to discover which agency you want to go with. Different agencies work in different areas in the world and in different ways and so you need to begin with prayer to really discern … yes okay I want to serve with God in this country or with this people group. Once you have established the country and people group, you need to begin gathering information and understanding that people group using different resources. Some people make the mistake of choosing an agency then decide where to serve, but God knows you best. He knows which people group will suit.

GAP YEAR

My husband and I decided we would travel. We wanted to visit different countries and people groups to see where we might serve. We had paid off our mortgage and raised our children except the youngest who was now finishing up in his last year of primary school. He was extremely young to go into high school so we thought a year of travel would help him mature. Our son thought a gap year was to do fun things like Disneyland and Legoland and so we thought we would do some of that too. Looking back now I guess maybe this approach was naïve or extravagant but that's what our thinking was at the time. It seems God had other ideas!

It was when I was praying about where we should go and how much time we should spend in each of these places, that I couldn't get past this country called Kazakhstan. I could barely even pronounce the name at the time, and I knew nothing about Central Asia, but I just kept thinking God wants us to stay in this country a little bit longer than the others. I wondered why. When I spoke to my husband he was sitting at his desk at the time, and he opened the top drawer and pulled out a flier and he said, 'This came in a couple of weeks ago, it's a job in Kazakhstan and I think it would suit us.' It was a missionary position with a missionary company and it fitted with what we thought we wanted to do. It was an administration position, and it went for a year, so we started down the path of going to meet with the agency and working through the process to go out on the field with this organisation. We learned God confirms our path to both of us, usually in different ways. Share your thoughts. Don't be afraid to speak out when you are unsure of the direction you are heading.

Looking at the fine print

When choosing an agency, read the mission statement and the core values of the agency carefully. Do they fit with your beliefs? Understanding this statement and values is vital because you are going to come under the authority of this agency and sign documents to agree with their practices.

This company that you have chosen and are going to have a long-term relationship with requires careful evaluation. Getting to know the culture of the organisation, not just talking to the person who is presenting information to you but also other people who are serving with this agency gives a better understanding of who they are. Asking questions is always a good way to get to know an agency, think of it as interviewing them. Asking a wide range of questions on their spiritual beliefs, family and children policies and even their dress code or bribery policy. What are their expectations of you? Scrutinising the details is a pain, but it is really very important because you don't know what's going to happen until it happens, so the more you are prepared the better.

CHANGING AGENCIES

My husband and I chose an agency that was associated with our church. We were happy the destination was where we thought God was sending us. To make sure, we travelled to the country to check out the school and meet the people we were going to be working with. Unfortunately, there was no room for us to stay in the agency's team-house, so we were housed at the Y base with a different organisation. This was not uncommon and often resources were shared. We enjoyed our host house, and they invited us to join them and work for their company, but we were happy with the agency we had already chosen. We returned home to finish our fundraising and were going through the process of getting all our documentation together and having our final medical check before heading out to our new country.

During a heart stress test the doctors discovered that my husband had a blockage in an artery, and it was decided to put a stent in which was done straight away. Afterwards he told the agency. Several weeks later we got a phone call from the agency and to our surprise we were told we were no longer able to be missionaries because the stent made my husband uninsurable. Of course, we were devastated because in our hearts we felt that God was sending us to this country and how could we not go! We had to take a step back and begin to pray and say well if you put this barrier in front of us Lord, what now? What do we do now? It is all in His timing. He had already gone before us and prepared the way. The organisation we stayed with when we visited the country were excited to have us join them. It took us another 12 months to return to our chosen country and when we did there was no room for us at the Y base, so we stayed in the team-house with our original organisation! God has a sense of humour. We learned it was okay to change direction, to change agencies and to gain different knowledge from another agency training.

What is the level of support?

Make sure you have a full understanding of the level of support the agency is going to provide. Some questions to consider include:

- Will they give you finances while you are on and off the field?
- What percentage goes to the agency and what comes to you?
- Do they have donors to help you raise support?
- Do they pay a wage? Insurance? Superannuation?
- Does the agency provide member care? Or can they access it through another source?
- Is anyone going to visit you from your agency while you are so far from home?
- Is there support for families with children? Day care? Extra financial assistance?

Support networks help you navigate the day-to-day challenges that can take your time away from your purpose, the reason you are there and doing what you are doing. It gets very lonely on the field if you don't have a support network.

Another important consideration is: what if there was an emergency in the country – what support (if any) will the agency provide for you?

THE RUSSIANS ARE COMING

We were in a situation in a country where the local people were afraid that there would be a Russian invasion. Russia bordered the country where we lived, and they had previously been part of the USSR. The threat felt real. While all the news was coming out in a foreign language, we felt lost. We wondered about our own security and of course that information or news was not getting through to the Australian media so no-one at home knew anything. Russia had invaded this country before, so the government was practising diplomacy, but the locals were afraid. What was our plan?

We began by speaking to our team leaders and trying to find a policy for the situation. There did not appear to be much of a plan, so we spoke to the agency; they didn't really have a strategic plan of getting us out of the country either. Next, we called our church and said what do we do? What should we do in this situation? It was very scary at the time. They could not help us. Having minimal answers from everybody we had asked we began to pray. Our first question was: should we stay or should we go? Is this a battle we are meant to be in? By this stage we had made many friends, so we did not want to leave. It is so difficult to know what to do when emotions are running high, so you need to already be prepared for these types of things in the event of an emergency. What are the resources available for you and your family? For us we had become very good *friends with an American organisation and they had a very good strategic plan for exiting the country. They had safe houses and so we were swept up in their exit strategy. We had to have a bag packed at the front door with our passport and documents, $600 American dollars and minimal clothing so that at a moment's notice we could leave the country or get to a safe house. As it happened, we didn't need an exit strategy – we were saved by the winter. It gets to -30 degrees during the winter, therefore there are never armed ground invasions in the cold. By spring the threat was over. Vladimir Putin had moved on to a different strategy.*

Questions

What if I don't know where I'm going?

If you are unsure which country you want to serve in, and don't know which type of people group you want to work with, I suggest you start by writing down what type of countries you like. Do you like a hot climate or a cold climate? Do you like to be by the sea, or do you like to be in the mountains? It's about personal preference. Do you want to live with a few people or a lot of people? Do you want to perhaps work in a Third World country, or do you want to work in a First World country?

Agencies

There are lots of different personal preferences in deciding where to work and once you've started to write down your likes and dislikes you will get a better picture. Praying about God's direction for you will bring clarity. God will place you in the right place. He is not going to send you somewhere that is not going to be good for you, so you need to trust the process.

Once you've worked out where in the world you want to go then you start to look at the agencies that work in that area and research them. Most agencies have a website so it's easy to access the mission statement. If reading and understanding a document is difficult for you then ask a friend to read it or a parent or youth leader. Someone who you have confidence in that can help you work out if that is something you believe. On the website there is always lots of information that will help you get a feel for the culture of the organisation. You can also view newsletters of others who are serving. Reading these letters may help formulate questions you can use when you interview the company.

How do I decide what level of support I need?

This is a big question, and I will say that it is never going to be perfect. How much support you require is personal choice. Some people really want to know all the details. Where they are going and how long it takes. They want everything to be put in place before they take the next step. They want to know where they are going to sleep, if they have a car, who they are going to be working with … they want to know all sorts of details. Other people are free spirited, they don't really care, they are not too fussed about what comes next, they just take it as it comes. They are not worried about the next meal or where they might sleep or whether they've got transport; they are more freelancers and just as happy to be in tune with the Holy Spirit. It's just a personal preference and neither is right or wrong. We are all different and so the level of support is often about what makes you comfortable.

Action Plan

Find a world map. Write a list of likes and dislikes of a few countries you know a little about.

Write down a few ideas about climate, geography and people groups. Begin to pray globally and see where God leads.

Research agencies through websites. Go along to their open nights. Ask questions. Talk to friends. Read newsletters from different organisations, different people groups and countries. You can never gather too much information.

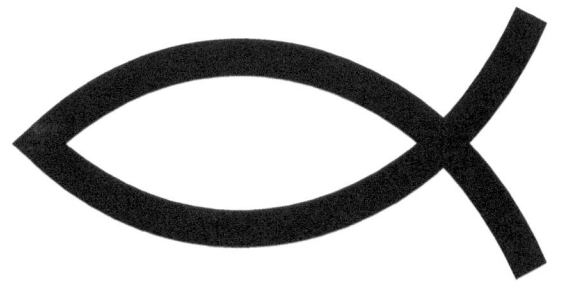

STEP 5

PRAYING

I guess as Christians we all know that there are many benefits to prayer. Prayer is not based on feelings; it's a state of mind. As the result of being in communication with God, we see prayers answered and the wonder of God turns into reality. So, it's a big part of our life. It's a big part of our beliefs. It's a big part of who we are, so it's invaluable to make prayer the most important part of our day. You cannot become a missionary unless prayer is central to your being. I cannot stress enough how you will totally depend on prayer daily when living as a missionary.

Prayer makes you alert. It makes you come alive, it makes you want to worship and above all it makes you want to spend more time with the one you love. Just like you want to eat your favourite food, you want to eat His word as Eugene Peterson[6] would say. I encourage you to make God come alive, begin each day in prayer, praise and worship. Thanking Jesus for all He is doing that day and ending the day in prayer thanking Him for every blessing for that day. In fact, you know, every time you pray regularly you are giving Him dominion over your life. This brings us to a state of alertness with the Lord.

Through prayer when we submit ourselves to the Lord, He releases His gifts to us. We do not feel as if we have any power, but when we come into His presence, it enables Him to flow through us. Raising us up so that we can be His hands and feet or salt and light in the community He has placed us in. We are confident to do what He asks. We have His blessing, if you like. Another way of saying it is you have spiritual authority and can exercise His power which comes through prayer. With authority to speak on His behalf you can go where others are afraid to go. It gives you confidence and encouragement knowing that He is with you. So even though it's frightening, even though you are filled with anxiety, it is the Holy Spirit's authority that enables you to go.

Prayer is also a place of refuge. When we really need to curl up and be loved. I think of it as being in a cocoon. Some people feel comforted in the arms of a lover or friend when they are hurting but we can also receive comfort from Jesus at times of stress or loneliness. A safe place to pray can be called a prayer closet, or some people feel close to God with worship music or wide-open spaces or a combination of several different stimuli. There are times when you have no space to be alone with God, you can only cover your head or close your eyes to find Him with you. If your relationship is strong, He will be with you whenever you call. You can even be close to Him in a room full of people. If you cry out, He'll find you. As a missionary you rarely get alone time, so it is good to practise being in the presence of Jesus no matter the situation, even if you don't have your Bible or music. The more you practise the easier it becomes. Find your mental cocoon so you can climb in at any time.

Some people in the world view prayer negatively. I guess sometimes people think that prayer is a cop-out. They might say, 'You must be a loser if you can't live in the world without some imaginary being holding your hand.' Overcoming this type of negativity sets you apart from the average person in the street. Turn the other cheek because it's not a part of who we are. Take a step in a different direction. You need to close your eyes with the ways of the world so that you can be a part of His plan. It is important to grow in reliance. If you do not get this prayer stuff and you try to go out in your own strength you will fail. There are a whole host of reasons why the Lord wants to walk with you. He wants you to hear him, he wants you to take it step-by-step in His time, to be obedient. Many people have come to me saying they were called to be missionaries, but it did not happen. Circumstances led them in a different direction. I believe it is because of their lack of relationship with God. Even if you feel God is taking you away from missionary work don't lose sight of the end goal; He hasn't.

I define prayer as adoration, a form of humbling ourselves before the king, to praise and worship God. It is also confession or giving thanks to God which is our primary act of communication. We are to ask and receive and knock so the door shall be opened. As it is written in Phil (4:6-7 NIV) 'Do not be anxious about anything, but in every situation, by prayer and petition, with thanksgiving, present your requests to God. And the peace of God which transcends all understanding, will guard your hearts and minds in Jesus Christ.'

Tony Glynn (1926–1994), an Australian Catholic missionary priest who worked in Japan played a crucial role in fostering international relations towards post-war reconciliation between Japan and Australia. He taught Bible studies, ran youth groups and organised aid deliveries from abroad.[7]

The miracle of prayer

Prayer is a miracle that happens between our conscious self and the unexplainable presence of God. Many people keep their visions and experiences with God a secret which makes it difficult to learn the art of transcending

Praying

into a type of paradise or union with God. This type of meditation comes from being still, something some of us have difficulty with. Not only is it being physically still but clearing our mind so it can be still too. This type of prayer can be frightening. It's overpowering as we gradually slip into an unconscious state. We are humbling ourselves to become a vehicle of His love. If you are around people who can hear God's voice, then ask them about what you are experiencing. God is consistent and persistent; He never gives up. He is always trying to communicate with us. If you hear the same message over time and in different ways, you are most likely hearing His voice, but test it with others and through scripture. Over time, through prayer, you will gain more confidence. The power and presence of God can totally transform our lives as this story shows.

SOLYA'S STORY

While in Central Asia with our 'Y' family we helped staff a DTS (Discipleship Training School). Usually, this school is for young people, but this group had a few more mature-aged students. One stands out. She was 56 at the time and an alcoholic. Her husband had tried everything to help her deal with her demons, but nothing worked. Eventually he let her go, and she wandered the streets in a drunken stupor. His love for her was not enough. Somehow, she found her way into our DTS. I have never seen the heart of a broken person so desperate for God's forgiveness. She spent hours and hours in prayer and never stopped crying. The program goes for 13 weeks and during this time I watched her transform both physically and emotionally. When she arrived, she wore odd socks, worn-out shoes, dirty clothes and had unloved hair. It was another person who came out the other side after 13 weeks. The second phase of the training is outreach. The students serve God by living and working in a different location. Solya embraced outreach with both hands. When it was over she knew she wanted to run her own church. An impossibility on so many fronts in a Muslim country. She was convinced this was God's plan for her life. We all shook our heads. This was not a good idea.

Within a year she had a building, and it was filled with the broken and lost just like she had been. She grew chickens which provided a source of income as well as feeding her flock. She learned to preach; God gave her a gift to speak to His people. She saw miracles and transformations so she loved to share with others. Soyla never stopped praying, she never stopped asking God what next. Unfortunately, a diagnosis of cancer is what came next. She told everyone in the hospital or wherever she could about Jesus and how he would heal her. This was a very brave act because any one of those people could have called the authorities, and she would have been jailed for sharing her faith in Christ. Solya was healed and the lord blessed her abundantly.

She spoke all over the city in underground churches and to anyone who would listen, raising money for her flock.

Once when she was talking to me, she asked if I had my own teeth. 'Yes', I replied. 'I'd like all my gold fillings removed so I could have nice teeth like yours,' she said to me. I was surprised by her request, but I could not think of how to help her. I should not have worried. I have no idea how, but God granted her heart's desire and the next time I saw her she had a mouth without gold.

Solya devoted the next few years to caring for others. Then after a brief illness, she passed away at the age of 61, but not before asking our team leader to give her a Christian burial. Her extended family stepped in and insisted on a traditional Muslim burial. Our team leader graciously stepped aside to allow the traditional funeral. He was then invited along with the members of her church to attend the ceremony. Our team leader's mother-in-law was a good friend of Solya and kept a record of all money the Christians gave to the family. The family were shocked at the generosity of Solya's friends. More importantly, Solya's family heard about her life with Jesus as testimony after testimony poured out of the mouths of the believers who attended the funeral. If Solya had had a Christian funeral none of her family would have attended and none of them would have heard her story of the loving God who transformed her life.

Building your prayer network

A prayer network is like building blocks. At first you learn to pray to God and so it becomes part of your DNA. Then find another person you are comfortable praying with. A person who you trust because this is about intimacy. It takes a long time to share your innermost feelings with someone so find a good friend to pray with. Your prayer partner will become essential when you are a long way from home because you need somebody who knows you very well. You don't want to share your personal feelings with just anyone. Sometimes you may have to ask God who this prayer partner is because you cannot visualise who you can trust to walk beside you in this journey. Equally, if you are a couple you still need to have a prayer partner. Most couples pray together and that is a good thing, but if you can find another prayer partner, preferably of the same sex, this will give you better support in the years to come.

Stage two in building your prayer team is to use what's available to you. Most churches have a prayer team who pray weekly for individuals in their church. Tell them of your desire to become a missionary and ask them to pray for you. Tell your family and your friends you need their support in prayer. Ask your small group or home group to pray for you. You might share your story with other small groups in your church and ask them to pray for you. Gathering prayer partners from different locations other than your church means these people are at arm's length from you. They may attend a different church or youth group. You might want to be in contact with them once a

Praying

week, so it is not as intimate as the one-on-one prayer person who supports you but more of a public type of prayer.

Starting a WhatsApp group is an easy way to connect. You can start a group with just a few and add others as they become interested. Give them a prayer update on a weekly basis so they know what to pray for, and know how you are feeling and what you are struggling with. This enables them to journey with you. It could be an interactive group, where they make their prayers for you public. Their interaction with you gives you encouragement. Alternatively, it could be a podcast, or you might put out a blog every week. There are many ways to communicate with people.

You could also use the agency if you have chosen one. They sometimes have a newsletter you could write an article in, which will be part of a wider network. By being part of their network, it opens your prayer circle. Newsletters are a traditional way missionaries communicate when they are overseas, but there is no reason you can't start writing for them before you leave home. Take every opportunity to speak at gatherings. In other churches, at conferences, at events – in doing so, you are extending your sphere of influence and taking people along with you on the journey. You are not alone on this journey. If you keep extending your network further, it allows you to appear larger. Your influence is larger, one step after another step. By allowing God's people to take this journey with you, they will be filled with joy. They love to hear what God is doing and how he is preparing you to go. They know they cannot go but they are excited to see you go.

OUR PRAYER TEAM

While my husband and I were on the field, we were very dependent on our prayer team in Australia. In Kazakhstan we lived and worked with our 'Y' family. We met with them every Monday morning for worship. We began praying for countries around the world. The locals led the worship time, and they liked to pray for neighbouring countries as well as their local community who were struggling. Their prayers became our prayer requests that we sent on to our prayer team and they would pray and sometimes shared a discerning message from God. This weekly ritual was a blessing for us because the more we stepped out in our Muslim country, the more we felt under attack. The prayer group became more vital for our wellbeing. We needed their discernment for what was happening around us.

We were not aware of the powers and principalities that were in the country when we arrived to begin work. We were naïve. It was not obvious at the beginning, but soon we realised there was a solid wall of resistance around us that could only be broken through prayer. We struggled to find our way. Geoff lost his driving licence, so I had to navigate the traffic, where it appeared there were no road rules. I just never looked in the rear-view mirror, never looked behind me! I didn't have an accident, God protected me. We didn't connect well with the local staff, who thought we wanted to take over leadership of the base which had never occurred to us. We were simply not interested, and *it took a couple of years before we conveyed that to them, and they could relax and become our friends. We did not fit in with the team we were allocated too. We had nothing in common and even though we tried our best, with frustration we began to work with others. It took a couple of years before our skills and abilities were recognised. We relied heavily on our prayer team back home because we wanted to be a blessing to others but there were many different relationships we encountered each day.*

I urge you to grow a spiritual base before you leave. One group or many groups praying for you is essential. It is much easier at this stage when you are in the comfort of your own home, and safe in familiar surroundings and you are not so dependent on prayer. Stretch your network as far and wide as possible.

Questions

What if I don't have anyone to pray with?

I guess this question is close to my heart because I didn't have anyone to pray with either. I did not feel confident about a one-on-one personal prayer partner. I thought it was enough to pray with my husband, as I didn't have another special person to pray with in my own country. Most missionaries I met while we were serving overseas did and I felt a pang of regret because I would have liked to have that support, so I urge you to share your inner self with a friend.

What if I don't know what to pray for?

This is often a difficult question. We don't want to just download our stuff on to God. We want to be guided by Him, we want Him to change our hearts to be more like Him. We want Him to put in our hearts the type of things He wants us to pray for. This may take a lifetime to achieve but is worth working on. Pray for things you are passionate about. Pray for things that just pop into your head. Pray for other's needs. As you practise, it will become easier and clearer what to pray for.

What if I don't feel any connection to God while in prayer?

Begin by reading the prayers emphasised in the bible. Remember the scriptures are written by the guide of the Holy Spirit and He is also our guide for the purpose of us to learn about God and to communicate with Him. Share with your one-on-one prayer partner your inner thoughts. Together you will discover a line of communication.

Praying

Action Plan

Talk to God about a prayer partner. Sometimes it's a leap of faith. Start by asking someone you trust to be your prayer partner or somebody God directs you to.

Read your bible with an emphasis on the devotional use of scripture.

Find new and creative ways to bring people into your world.

Another step would be journaling. Start writing regularly and once you've got answers from God then you'll get excited about writing every day. If you stay focused and write it down, you will not forget the wonderful things God is doing because sometimes our memories fail us. If you write it down and God answers, you'll see His faithfulness.

STEP 6

MOULDING

Why change? Do you have to change? You may not have to change how you do things or how you think, but our world is rapidly changing around us. Dealing with change successfully is a learned skill that is useful to have in our armour. You may want to put the changes you are facing into perspective. Will it affect me in years to come? Think about the risk to change versus reward to change. Change is a big part of life because it is going to happen anyway. The world continues to change – either we change with it, or we do not.

Technology for instance, is continuing to evolve. We are always learning new things to keep up with the changes. Mobile phones were born in 1973. The mobile phone service began in Australia in 1981. Ray Tomlinson is generally credited with the first email in 1971 between two different computers. Who knew the impact of Covid 19 before it began in 2019. Or Zoom which began its journey in April 2011. It was because of Covid 19 and our isolation that we all know how to use Zoom. All these technical things changed our lives. Most of us find personal change difficult, but resisting change does not allow God to work in us. Resisting change is very common. We are capable of so much more than we can imagine. Sometimes we are unaware that we have a resistance to something new. Think about what your life might look like if you could embrace changes. If you could see the benefits in changing your world view. How we view the world around us often determines our resistance to change. Sometimes it is helpful if someone can show us what change might look like.

In Jeremiah we see a great example of God showing us about change. Jeremiah, 18:3-6: 'So I went down to the potter's house, and I saw him working at the wheel. But the pot he was shaping from clay was marred in his hands; so, the potter formed it into another pot, shaping it as seemed best to him. Then the word of the Lord came to me. He said, "Can I not do with you Israel, as this potter does?" declares the Lord. "Like clay in the hands of the potter, so are you in my hands, Israel."'

As God begins moulding you in his image, allow your true self to come through. You need to manage these changes;

Moulding

you must integrate change into your life in ways that work for you so that it gives you confidence. Moulding makes you more in tune with your journey. In tune with God's plans for you. God will continue to mould you as you go onto the field. It is a lifelong commitment. We are never going to be perfect. Often, we get it wrong. There is always more to learn.

We need to change responsibly. You need to stay true to yourself and to your beliefs. You can change your strategies, but your principles are the rudimentary core of your being. It is vital you understand who you are in Christ because that will be challenged many times in your journey. Knowing who you are and what you believe affects the way you deal with change and will enhance your lifestyle. If you are unsure and have not made a conscious decision about your beliefs, you will not be able to change effectively.

I think growth is exciting, when we embrace it. We become motivated to do more in our lives. You develop creative solutions by becoming flexible. It is a new mindset. Being flexible is one of those positive things you can bring to your team when you are on the field. When you embrace change it attracts new opportunities, they seem to come from nowhere. Something that was a problem now becomes an opportunity. Doors open for you. It is a unique feeling once you have embraced the idea of change. People often feel more compassionate when they grow accustomed to change.

Some people get stuck or trapped in a notion that God has forgotten them, or they are waiting on God to do something.

This is not an uncommon thought. God wants to change us, mould us and move us in a particular direction, but we can be stubborn. You can be walking in a particular direction, and you think everything looks good. Ten years pass and nothing has changed from that initial spark from God. You wonder what happened. You may feel fatigue, apathy, stress, loss of control or let down by God. Some people keep waving their hands in the air, 'I'm still here God!' All sorts of heaviness comes on you because you know something needs to change.

Sophia Blackmore (1857–1945) was sent by the Methodist Women's Foreign Missionary society to work in Singapore. She helped found two Christian schools for girls. Sophia also helped establish a boarding school supported by the early Methodist Straits Chinese Christian work and published a periodical in Baba Malay.[8]

The world is constantly changing and evolving. We are either going with it or we are going against it. If we are going with it, we are growing. If we are resisting, our world gets smaller. It begins to decay. If we remain stagnant, we are really going backwards. Embrace a bigger picture by managing change. It is a learned skill which we can all learn at any age. As a people group, we continually evolve. As a person, do not ever sit still, continue to give yourself challenges in life. This makes you feel as if you have had a successful life.

Embracing new ideas

Ideally, we would like change to happen slowly, allowing ourselves time to try new things. Sometimes we are unable to control change, it comes at us, and we have no control over it, but we always have the power in the way we respond. Instead of reacting to somebody's comment or something you find hurtful at the time, resist the temptation to engage in that battleground, resist the temptation to get hooked into that fight. Learn to surrender. If it is something important you can go back once the heat of the moment is over. This may be a new concept for you.

On the other side of the coin are the people pleasers, who quite often walk away or instantly surrender. But we all need to try again, to come back sometime later to resolve the issue. To perhaps look at a different point of view and be willing to change our position a little and meet them halfway. We need to search within ourselves to step out of our comfort zone. Maybe you need to open that door slowly. It takes time, it is not easy to make changes. But it is possible to change how you react to different situations. It is often a good idea to choose something that you feel you can accomplish to gain confidence, and then allow the momentum to propel you forward. You know, walking 1000 km starts with one step. Do not look all the way forward, just move one step at a time. This allows you to achieve success. If we learn to lean on the Lord, He will show us a way forward.

TO BE A CHEERFUL GIVER

Many years ago, I was not a generous person. I had trouble tithing. I wanted to know all the details of where the money was going and so on. I thought I was being a good steward, but in fact I had a lesson to learn.

The Lord asked me to put $200 into a plain white envelope with no identification so no-one would know who sent it and place it in a particular letterbox in our street. I thought it was my imagination, so I forgot about it. Three weeks later I got the same message. I argued with God, 'But this was more than 10% of my income, it's half! How would I feed my children and pay my bills?' I complained. This is not a word from God, I argued with myself.

Two weeks later I arrived at my local primary school to collect the children and there was a great commotion. One of the mothers was telling the story about how she went to her letterbox and found $200 in a plain white envelope. I said nothing and went home in tears. I had not been obedient. I had known God was speaking to me, but

I chose to turn away. When I told my husband what had happened, he said I should fulfil what the Lord had asked me to do. Reluctantly, with a heavy heart, I placed $200 in a plain white envelope and placed it in the letterbox. I was very proud of myself thinking I had done a good deed. I spent the day patting myself on the back. I went as usual to school to collect my children and again there was a great commotion. This time the mum was in tears. She was a single mum with four children, and she was worried someone was watching the house and they were in danger. I said nothing and again went home in tears. I humbled myself and repented before God.

A couple of weeks passed. As usual I collected my son from school when I saw the single mum with four children wearing a lovely new hairstyle and waving tickets to a concert. I was furious, how could she use that money for luxury items instead of something that is important, like food or bills. Eventually when I calmed down, I began to pray. The Lord said, 'You gave me the money to do with it as I please'. For the remainder of the year, He encouraged me to give away money to all sorts of people, charities and events. We never went hungry; the bills were always paid, and we never went without. I changed and learned many valuable lessons that year.

You need to own the changes you make. It is important that you own the decisions you make. Do not feel the changes are put upon you. It needs to be a light-bulb moment or a revelation, something to embrace, not a thing being forced upon you. God never forces us to do anything that we do not want to do. He has given us a free will, so feel free to use it. This allows the change to happen in your time. He knows what needs to be changed, He knows how to change things. You just need to be responsible in the way in which you embrace change.

Be prepared, as you will come under attack. The enemy does not want you to change, because the change in you brings you closer to God. As you get closer to God and what He wants for you then the attacks will come harder and faster and more often. So you need to be prepared for the enemy. A leopard never changes his spots or the methods he uses to deceive us. Keep your eyes focused on Jesus as you are going through this process of change. By sharing your thoughts and concerns with your one-on-one prayer partner he/she will be constantly looking out for the enemy. This is one of those times when having a close relationship is helpful.

Flexibility is a learned skill

How does a person cope with changes in circumstances? A flexible person can adapt quickly to new situations. They can think outside the square. They are versatile and can think of alternatives easily. Flexibility is a fundamental component of missionary life. You are going to be in places and situations on many occasions where you just do not know what is in front of you or how you are going to deal with it. You must trust the process. The process is to go with the flow. Allow God to work in all situations. To accomplish change requires strong spiritual dependency on God. Be influenced by Him in all you do. God never asks us to do the big things, He always asks us just to do little steps that are doable and within our capabilities. If you just allow yourself to accept these little steps, then you can accomplish things that you never thought possible. I just ask that you focus on His voice and His encouragement and His teachings. This will help you grow spiritually.

WILL'S STORY

Our teenage son lived with us when we were on the field. On Friday nights he would have his friends over and they would hang out and have fun. Most of the time we were home upstairs leaving the young people to make pizzas and play their music. But on this night we were not home. There was a loud knock at the front door and our son opened it. To his surprise there were two large 6-feet 6-inch Russian soldiers standing tall. They asked to see our papers. Our son said in English his parents were not home, and he did not know where the papers were. The soldiers spoke little English, some of the youth started using the few Russian words they knew but this didn't help. Our son then invited them in for pizza and to wait until his parents returned. The soldiers tried hard to intimidate him, but he just used the opposite spirit. The soldiers had no authority over the young people. They continued to be all smiles and offering

> *food and drink which completely changed the situation. The soldiers' intimidating tactics did not work and they left shaking their heads.*

When there is a change in you and the way you approach life, people will see the change and they will become excited, and gather around you. They will feel the excitement within you, they will see something is different, they will see that your focus is different. They will notice things about you that they had not noticed before. Even though you have had these things hidden under a rock for many years, it will become evident. The changes will become obvious. The Holy Spirit brings with it a gathering of people. People who want to get on board with what Jesus is doing. This is an exciting time, a very exciting time and you will look at problems differently. You will look at solutions instead of problems, so you will become the person that God wants you to be. Isn't that what we all want, to become who God wants us to be? Only you and God know what needs to change.

TRAINING CAMP

> *I saw the most change in people and myself during our training camp to go overseas as missionaries. We met in a large campsite, high up in the forest. I remember one morning coming to breakfast and one of the wives Jane*

was looking for her husband Dennis. His Bible and gloves were on the table, but he was nowhere to be found. Another person was looking for her daughter – she seemed to have vanished. Shortly after I sat down to breakfast, our camping site was surrounded by masked men holding guns. They told us several people from our camp had been taken and we needed to follow them if we wanted to see them again.

We were herded in the direction of three large bunk bedrooms at the back of the campsite and divided up – men in one room, women in another and children in the third. Several hours passed. Someone came to the door and demanded we choose two hostages to go free. We made decisions based on people's marital status and age of children, etc. We thought to ourselves this must be a training session, but it felt real and threatening. Several hours passed before someone returned to say our government was not negotiating with them so the two we had chosen would be shot. They then asked who the two people were who had been chosen. As quick as a flash a woman stepped forward and said she was one of the chosen when in fact she was not, but she had never married, and she was willing to sacrifice herself. Almost at the same time, another woman stepped forward who also had not been chosen by the group but was willing to sacrifice herself as well. She was much older and had decided her children were now old enough and her husband could take care of the family. They left our bunk room. We were not told anything further. We heard lots of shouting in foreign languages and loud banging on the walls of our bunk room, then several gunshots and silence. The women I was with were fearful for the children and their husbands and it was difficult to control our emotions with common sense.

A while later we were all released – the 'exercise' was over, and we had time to reflect on the situation that was presented to us. We discovered afterward the children were released immediately and returned to the camp to enjoy lots of fun activities without their parents. We also discovered the older woman who left our bunk room to sacrifice herself was confronted with her husband who had also offered to sacrifice himself. While their children may have been grown up, they would have lost both parents. The exercise challenged us to make decisions quickly and to think through the decisions we were making. Many of us had to change the way we made decisions.

Questions

What if I tried and failed to change?

Start with something small. What might be small for me may be big for you. But let's say you pray every morning that you are a blessing to everyone you meet that day. You begin by smiling at people and making polite conversation. As you do this you gain confidence and people feel confident to interact with you. People begin to feel good when they

Moulding

see you and this brings positive energy around you. That is probably the best way to begin your changes. If you take the time to practise, you will get results. Once you have gained confidence in an area, it gives you strength to move on to the next one.

What if I tried to change in the past?

If you feel you have failed at something you have tried to change, then you need to try a different approach. Try something new, think about how to do it differently. Preparing for change helps us feel in control. Just like preparing for an event, an exam or an interview. Create areas in your life where there is little change, safe spaces so you can cope with changes in other areas. For example, the physical surroundings of your home may remain constant which allows other areas of your life to change more quickly without you feeling as if you have lost all control.

What if I forget and slide back to doing things in the old way?

Allow God to do the work for you. Be open to God, it is a simple prayer: 'God show me what it is that needs to be changed.' We all need to lean on God in relation to change because many times we are unable to see what needs to change or we are incapable of changing it in our own strength. A strong spiritual dependence on Jesus in our lives keeps us grounded. It has been the stabilising influence in my life that has got me through many changes that I would have thought were impossible.

Action Plan

Write your changes in your prayer journal. Small changes lead to bigger changes. Pray and write every step. The expectations and the results you have are important to journal. You will see these things answered through your journaling.

Something to practise – try intentionally allowing a different approach to an event. Maybe let a member of your family or work colleague lead on something when normally you might lead. Alternatively, take the lead yourself if this is unfamiliar to you. When the plans change, or they are challenged, try going with the flow. Take a deep breath and try to enjoy the new experience. Most things are not life or death events, they are just changed circumstances.

STEP 7
FUNDRAISING

Raising funds is a process, to gather contacts with churches and others. Gathering financial contributions voluntarily through individuals, businesses, by pledging, garage sales, bake offs, any type of event. It is only limited by your imagination.

The question of finance is always a challenge for every missionary. It is not a subject that we feel confident about discussing. There is a reward for raising money – you get to serve God, and the people in the church who cannot go get to see God work through you. One of the biggest myths is the fear of rejection. Most missionaries do not like putting themselves out there. They are ashamed to ask for money. God has already gone before you because in the Bible there are examples of people being paid for ministry. Paul describes (1 Cor 9:1-18 NIV) why he has the right to receive financial support from other Christians. He does not want to charge people to hear the gospel, but he has a right to eat and drink and take a wife like everyone else. So, asking for money is not a new concept, but it is the same struggle every generation who goes out to do ministry has. We all struggle with the same fear of rejection which causes stress and anxiety. But it is not wrong to ask for money.

Our background regarding money influences our way of thinking about money. Our childhood and culture shape our attitudes and behaviour around money. Positive messaging in our youth like saving, budgeting and spending responsibly contribute to how we deal with finance as adults. We are also influenced by the media, friends and family. We sometimes create a glass ceiling around our abilities to achieve our financial goals. All these different influences contribute to the way in which we ask for money. This affects the way we do ministry, evangelism and mission. We all have a money personality. You might play it safe with your finances and only invest in low level risk investments or you may like to take high risks with your finances and live on the edge – or anywhere in between. There is no right or wrong attitude to finance. We are all just different.

Raising support is an ongoing process. It is something that needs to be attended to on a regular basis. There are different types of people who want to give money to you for different reasons. For example, there's the Sower who wants to support you as you go out. It is helpful to understand the different ways people are involved in the giving process and how you might approach them. There are others who want to wait to see if you get onto the field before they begin to support you. There are still others who want to support projects, events or activities. Some have a desire to support church planting or orphans. We do not often know why people support us, we just need to continue to ask the question.

It is important to have some control over your finances – you need to take responsibility for your living costs while you are away. Even if you are with an agency that has all your money in their control, everything is fluid and at any stage a supporter may drop out if their situation changes, so you will be short of funds. It happens often. Agencies adjust, but eventually it comes back on your shoulders. Leaning on God in prayer is always our first step. We are dependent on Him for guidance. Knowing how to 'drought proof' your finances as I call it, enables you to carry on with your ministry. Being prepared for all situations helps you have control. It is one of our fears that we will find ourselves abroad without any money.

We first seek the kingdom of God, not the money. We care about the relationships we have with people before we care about their potential contributions. God promises to provide all our needs. When money is our first thought, everything we do is tainted by that thought. Whereas our first thought should be our love for Jesus and loving one another, and everything we need will be added. As God leads us in building relationships with people, we are given opportunities to share our ministry with them. The life of a missionary is all about giving and receiving. We learn to give generously; we learn to receive with humility; we learn the value of friendship. We have learned that friendship and sharing our lives with others helps us mentally and emotionally. It also helps us stay grounded to our home country and to our church and family.

Charles Brooking Hannah (1874–1961), or 'Brook' as he was known, played Australian rules football with Carlton. He was inspired by Hudson Taylor's call for young men to serve for 5 years without thought of marriage. He joined the China Inland Mission as an ordained missionary and survived the attack on foreign missionaries during the boxer rebellion where many Christians died.[9]

HE PROVIDES

My husband, son and I had a format for speaking at churches. My husband provided the facts, I provided the emotion, and our son provided the humour. I remember speaking in a country church and everything went perfectly. We all played our part, and all the technology worked. Unfortunately, we did not receive any support from the church or individuals. The following week we spoke in another country church, and nothing worked. The sound from the video did not match the picture. I lost my concentration while speaking and messed up the cues for the others to speak and so on. What a disaster. That church became one of our best supporters. They were excited to see us every time we were back in the country. The lesson we learned from that day was it was not about what we did or how we did it, but it was about what God does. We continue to give Him the glory for all that He does. He provides all our needs.

The traditional way to raise financial support is by travelling around to visit churches, where we begin gathering people to accompany us on the journey. It works in the same way you build a prayer network, but instead you are building a financial base. The people in the church where you speak expect you to ask for financial support. They know how the system works. The pastor would not have invited you to speak unless he/she was happy for you to ask for money. Once you have spoken from the front you will be accepted by the congregation. It is then possible to move into the smaller groups that usually gather weekly or every two weeks in the homes of church members. This is a very good place for you to meet face-to-face with individuals and become connected with the whole church. Following up with a newsletter helps to stay in touch long after you have first connected with them. It helps you to take them on the journey with you.

WATERMELON STORY

My husband and I spoke in a Slavic church hoping to raise support. The church had not supported us, but several individuals did. We were regularly invited back to speak. One time we arrived expecting to speak but they had forgotten they invited us. They were having what they called 'first fruits day' to celebrate the harvest. They give the first fruit of the season to God. The church hall was loaded with all the fruit and vegetables harvested at the beginning of the season, and they were offering it to God. It was a carnival atmosphere. We joined in the festivities of laughter and ate masses of food. They were selling food to one another to raise money. Small bags of vegetables and fruit like tomatoes or olives for ridiculous amounts of money. It was a fun way to make donations. We were told all the funds were going to missions. A competition was held for the biggest watermelon of the season. The watermelon had the current year carved into it. I expect that was so you could not win with the same melon every *year! The watermelons were weighed then auctioned – some sold for $200-$300. It was a fun day. We shared a story of our work in central Asia with Russian mothers and all the proceeds raised were given to us. God had placed us in that church at that time for His purpose. We were faithful and obedient.*

We need to understand our supporters. God likes a cheerful giver. We have all heard that before – it is used often in sermons when asking for money and it is true. Many times, we forget that people enjoy giving in all sorts of different ways, especially Christians. They know that they cannot go so they want to send you. People know you cannot go unless you have the money and so you need to have that in the back of your mind. People want to give you money!

There are several different types of people who are going to give you money. Some people want to help you get started or get your project off the ground. This is called seed money. Like a startup fund. Another type of person that will give you money is somebody who understands that you need a stable cash flow. Sometimes for the life of your mission trip, or sometimes for a set period. These people may pay you monthly or quarterly or even annually. We once had someone give us 10% of his lawn mowing business. We watched over time how much his business grew.

There is yet another group of people who will give for a project. We once asked for $1200 for the repairs of a van we used on outreach all the time. We got an overwhelming response – enough to buy a new van. Some friends of ours had a fun idea. A family we knew were specifically looking for funds to fly somewhere. Their children created a model airport with lots of homemade planes. It sat in the foyer of the church where people were able to pledge money for the flight. Many of us will have seen the thermometer that is a really popular way to raise money. The idea is to have a picture of a thermometer going up as you raise more money. It is a visual aid which helps remind people of your target. There are lots of different ways to ask for money. It is only limited by your imagination.

The only thing the Lord is asking you to do is put aside your fears. Give Him your fears and allow Him to open the doors into the networks that He has for you. Ask yourself where are your spheres of influence? Think about the networks you already have. Your church of course is one avenue, small groups are another, work, family and friends are another. Try expanding those networks by inviting people to your place and asking them to bring a friend. Someone new you have not met before, maybe from another church. Embrace hospitality with regular events at your place or the park or the church. Cultural nights with food from the country you intend to serve are always a fun way to engage people.

When I was thinking about a marketing strategy for a friend of mine, to help them to get onto the mission field, I thought I would use the networks I had in my own state to raise funds because it was familiar, but the door shut quickly. As I was praying about it the Lord said, 'Cast the net on the other side of the boat.'(John 21:6 NIV). So I went back into my friend's state and doors began to open. It was much easier for her to visit locations in her own state. God always has a much better plan than I do.

Prayer is always your number one go-to place for ideas and guidance. After all, He wants you on the field sharing the gospel. On the other hand the enemy does not, so expect all manner of distractions. The thing I found interesting was when I sowed in one paddock, I sometimes reaped in another. There were times we would speak in a tiny little church out in the middle of nowhere. We were being obedient to what we felt God wanted and often there were times we thought there was no result, only to discover that God had given us a great blessing from an unexplained source. It would roll in from places we had no idea about, no connection to, with no understanding where or why it was coming to us. What I learned was money was no problem to God. If we were obedient and went where we were asked to go, where we were invited to go, where God encouraged us to go, then the money would come. We just needed to put one foot in front of the other and not be afraid. Being fearful just gives the enemy an open door. You do not want to give him an inch.

The future of mission work is changing

Individuals, churches and charities are no longer looking to fully fund work in missions abroad. God is still calling people to be missionaries, however, the way it is done is changing. Years ago, among the farming population, it was said if a farmer married a teacher, they would have a successful farm. A teacher would provide a steady income stream to support the family throughout the year and the farm income that only came in once or twice a year provided for big expenses as well as the running and upkeep of the land. Today many farms have several wind generators on the farms that provide a secondary income. That gives the farm stability which is what they call 'drought proofing'. In apostle Paul's day, he asked to share in the harvest of those who followed Christ and wrote letters to churches asking for support. He also believed in supporting himself. In the scripture in Acts 18:1-18, Paul meets Aquila and Priscilla who own a tent-making business. He is happy to work in a business that is not a ministry to receive an income. When the need arises, Paul will work to support himself. This is where the expression 'tent making' comes from, which means working in the community in which you live. He was not reliant on just one source of income. He used his skills or learnt new ones for whatever God provided.

I had a friend who began a popcorn business in the country where he served, which employed many locals. It not only provided income for his family, a wife and six children, but also showed Christ in action through the work practices of the business. He was also a teacher in the school his children attended. He did an amazing job. It was a good example of work life and ministry balance. For the modern missionary we need to be creative in the ways we support ourselves. Many missionaries work as teachers or in the medical field in the country they serve in. Today with the technology that is available there are many ways to have secondary incomes.

In conclusion, we need both. We may need to be self-reliant and find paid work to support our everyday needs. I think the local people in the country you serve in like to see you are working alongside them. The church and the individuals who support you like to see we are contributing to our own life and not just having a free ride. For some people who only want to focus on ministry it can be frustrating, but we also need to see God in action.

The awesomeness of what God does just blows your mind – and who would want to miss out on that? I am still excited when I see God move, even after all these years. You would think by now I would learn to expect it, but it is still a buzz. When I was living only by faith, I likened it to walking on water. There was no safety net. We felt like the most blessed people in the world. How we managed to travel all over the world and stay in lovely houses, own a car, even take holidays while serving Jesus was incredible. How God provided us with paid work and a free apartment was unbelievable.

Questions

What if I just do not want to raise funds?

The simple answer to that is to choose an agency that pays all your expenses. There are some agencies that pay a wage and all associated costs. There is a whole lot of criteria which goes with an organisation that provides that level of support. The agency may require a higher education than other agencies. They will have much more control over you. There will be a system, and you will need to comply with the way things are done. These agencies are developed over many hundreds of years and for some stepping into that type of world is perfect. Everything has been prepared ahead of time so there are no surprises. Your destination and how you will serve has all been arranged.

What if I have tried to raise funds in the past but I have been unsuccessful?

You need a new strategy or inspiration. If possible, talk to other people who have been successful at raising support. Do not sit on the issue or avoid it and hope it goes away. Ask for help. Find someone who is a good organiser and understands marketing strategies and get a plan. You have a team of people praying for you – ask if there is someone who could help you put a plan together. God does not expect you to be able to do all things so He will put people around you who can guide you. You are not alone on this journey.

What if I forget to ask for money when I am speaking to people?

In Betty Barnett's book *Friend Raising*[10] she talks about building a missionary support team that lasts. She focuses on the idea of growing relationships or developing friendships rather than raising money. As you are raising friendships and building relationships, it will eventually bring in the money and all sorts of other support. Prayer and journaling will overcome fear. Understanding the joy of the giver will help keep you motivated. As Betty said, 'I had a close friend who did not financially support me, and I did not know why. One day I got up the courage to ask. She said, "I have been hurt because you have never asked me to financially support you." It was a good lesson for me.'

Action Plan

Discover what your money personality is, so you are more aware of how you think about money.

Read books and listen to podcasts to get inspired.

Get excited about where you are going and what you are going to do once you are on the field. Focusing on these things will make you have a bubbly, inspirational personality. It will flow out from you and that will help you when you're raising money.

Get organised with a marketing plan. With a newsletter you will need a spreadsheet with names, email addresses, church attending, etc. Mailchimp or another type of mailing system which has reminders and follow-up appointments are great systems to have in place.

Always share your journey with your prayer team.

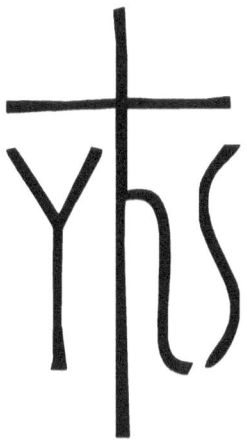

STEP 8

YIELDING

This part of your journey is deeply personal. The intimacy you have with God depends on how much time you have with Him and how much you allow him into your life. Hearing God's voice enables you to be guided, loved, encouraged and comforted by Him. There is a richness in the quality of our lives when God is part of it. You cannot make this connection any other way than through Jesus. Embrace His love, surrender to it, enjoy it. Yielding gives us freedom from carrying the load because Jesus now carries the burden for us. In scripture we read 'Come to me, all who are weary and burdened, and I will give you rest. Take my yoke upon you and learn from me, for I am gentle and humble in heart and you will find rest for your souls. For my yoke is easy and my burden is light.' (Matthew 11:28-30 NIV) This is an invitation from Jesus.

Sometimes we see people weighed down with the weight of the world on their shoulders. This is not God's intention. Yielding gives us freedom from wrongdoing or condemnation because there is nothing that we have done that does not come under the grace of God. This quote from Eugene Peterson, from his book *A Long Obedience in the Same Direction*, exemplifies the enemy:

> 'The lies are impeccably factual. They contain no errors. There are no distortions or falsified data. But they are lies all the same, because they claim to tell us who we are and omit everything about our origins in God and our destiny in God. They talk about the world without who made it. They tell us about our bodies without telling us they are temples of the Holy Spirit. They instruct us in love without telling us about the God who loves us and gave Himself for us.'[11]

Let's not focus on our faults or our brokenness, but instead, on the grace God shows us.

Paul writes in scripture 'repentance from dead works' (Heb 6:1). Again, he says in Hebrews 'How much more, then, will

Yielding

the blood of Christ, who through the eternal Spirit offered himself unblemished to God, cleanse our consciences from acts that lead to death so that we can serve the living God!'(Heb 9:14) We all need to declutter at times, both internally and externally. Cleansing our souls, purifying our hearts, is an act to rid ourselves of impure thoughts leading to actions or deeds. Usually, we can identify our own sins easily but sometimes there are subtle sins we are unaware of. Just ask God, 'What are my sins?' Give Him permission to show you what needs to be addressed.

Yielding gives you the freedom that comes from relinquishing all your stuff. This is more than decluttering your life. Giving up all your safety nets is a real challenge and quite an achievement. We must do this before going onto the field. Giving up our creature comforts is not done lightly. We do not realise how much having an income, having a house, our own furniture, car and personal possessions mean to our wellbeing. We are told by society all these things we put in place provide us with security and safety. As a society we rely on systems and technology to help us keep up with the pace of life. Where does your security lie? Can you give it all up?

According to the *Baptist Press*, 'One of the reasons missionaries leave the field is due to conflict with other missionaries. After many years of training, equipping and sacrifice they are unable to work together.'[12] None of us are perfect but this sounds like an attack from the enemy to me. Divide and conquer is one of his methods for preventing God's work. It means learning how to overcome resistance.

We have all been challenged with resisting the devil's ways in various forms. This enemy of God will try anything to throw you off course. Be prepared, the closer you get to your due date for departure the harder the forces will conspire against you. Stay close to God. The *Baptist Press* goes on to conclude, 'Missionaries must intentionally pursue intimacy with Christ and learn to abide in Him long before they ever cross geographical, cultural and linguistic barriers.'[12]

By being obedient and submissive to His word, a yielding person can change the way they normally do things or deal with situations. It is helpful to be flexible. A yielding person may submit to arguments, demands or pressure. This may sound like a weak person but actually they are strong. There are times to stand firm, but always look for a way to resolve issues that arise as they inevitably will. Be a good communicator.

Fred and Betty Evans served in Papua New Guinea between 1976–2004. They said, 'Missionaries are a unique group of people in that they seldom seek recognition preferring rather to be about their "Father's" business without fanfare or glory.'[13]

Connecting to God

There is always a struggle between the way we do things and the way God does things. The more we get to know Jesus through His word, the more we understand the Father. If you want to serve God, allow Him to place His desires in your heart. That means approach Him with empty hands and allow Him to fill you up with the Holy Spirit. If we come to Him with preconceived ideas, we are not yielding to God. Sometimes we go to God with our plans for Him to bless them. He will often honour our desires but if we surrender to Him, we get so much more than we can even imagine. As in scripture James 4:7-8 NIV: 'Submit yourselves, then, to God. Resist the devil, and he will flee from you. Come near to God and He will come near to you. Wash your hands, you sinners, purify your hearts you double-minded.' It does not need to be complicated. Keep it simple. Humble yourself before the Lord. Allow Him to guide you.

We connect with God through reading the Word, talking to Him in prayer or singing His praises in worship. He may also connect with us by sending a godly person into our lives. He may reach us through an angel or dreams and visions, through circumstance and inner peace and conviction. The Lord is always trying to seek us out. He is not sitting on His throne on high being distant from us. He desires a relationship. Always be on the lookout for a sign from God.

We often suffer from resistance to a relationship with God.

Why? We are a mixture of both conscious and unconscious minds. A balance between the two. The conscious mind is level-headed, sensible, reasonable and logical. The subconscious is all about heart, emotions, memory, beliefs and intuition. However, there is a third level of consciousness that connects us to God. We often find our will, our head, and the desires of our heart pushing in different directions. We put up barriers, so we are unable to reach this place between the conscious and unconscious mind.

For example, what if you and I spoke different languages? Our conscious mind would find a way to overcome the barrier enabling us to communicate with each other. What if in my subconscious mind I felt guilty for not being able to speak to you in your language? My conscious mind does not want to admit it and tries to separate itself from the subconscious mind. Similarly, if our beliefs are challenged by what we see or understand then a barrier goes up, if we do not think it through. The conscious mind is speaking but the unconscious mind is not listening. On a spiritual level, God is always communicating with us on a subconscious level, but we may choose on a conscious level not to hear because a barrier stops us hearing God's voice. God does not stop talking, but we are not always hearing.

ART THERAPIST

Over many years I have learned to be obedient to God. Usually, I can follow His lead but this request from God came as a complete surprise. This happened to me when we were missionaries in Latvia. It is a funny story to me because God put in my heart to be an art therapist. I laughed at His suggestion because I thought I had no artistic creativity in me. I cannot draw or paint, but God knew I was obedient. I took an online course for 6 weeks; it was a quick course and gave me an idea of what to do. I had a very good friend who was an art therapist, and while we were in Australia I went along to do some of her classes and that gave me some more ideas. Once I returned to Latvia. I said to my team that I felt that I was to do art therapy. 'That is interesting,' they said, 'because Latvia is culturally artistic.' What was also interesting was art therapy classes were starting to appear in all sorts of locations in the capital city of Riga. Our agency's national director told me a woman had come across from the USA 10 years before, believing God told her the Latvians would come to know the gospel through art therapy. These bits of information encouraged me.

I prayed and I waited to see where God wanted me to serve. Nothing, a total blank. I walked, read my bible, prayed, prayer walked throughout the city to see where God might lead me. Nothing. For weeks I waited on God. Doubts crept in. I prayed against the enemy; guilt made me question this idea I had in my head. Eventually I felt God wanted me in the women's prison. The previous year I had served with an international women group in the prison in a section for mums and babies. We took the children out of the prison on excursions and bought gifts for them like shoes and gloves. Now God was asking me to go into the same prison unit and do art therapy with that group of women whom I had never met, only their children. I told my co-workers, and they all made suggestions of the contacts they could introduce me to, such as the chaplain or the social worker who worked at the prison, but I felt that was not right. I did not have a sense of peace about their suggestions.

I prayed every day that God would open the right door. What was the right door to open? Again, I felt self-doubt and guilt because people were paying for me to be in the country and all I was doing was hanging out with God in prayer and worship. Maybe I was overthinking this, maybe I should just go with the avenue of the social worker or chaplain? Waiting on God seemed like forever.

Eventually a shy woman who was one of my teammates came to me and said she had a friend who goes into the women's prison every Sunday afternoon to do Bible studies. It was the same unit with mothers and babies. Immediately I knew this was the door I had been waiting for. Christinia was part of a Russian church. She and four others had been visiting the women's prison every

Yielding

Sunday for years. I met with her, and we got on like a house on fire even though she only spoke Russian and my Russian was pitiful. Our mutual friend translated for us, and I used the little Russian I had, and she used the little English she had, and we connected. She began with the paperwork required for me to come into the prison with her team. Meanwhile God was gathering a team of people around me. Firstly, God brought me a translator, somebody who could speak Latvian, Russian and English and then there was an artist who became friends with me who was interested in coming into the prison. The pace began to pick up. I felt energised.

My teammates began to pray and ask excitedly at our gatherings what was happening next. The prison authorities granted us permission to enter the prison. We began doing art therapy with the women. It was effective, and they responded well to me. I am sure it is because I was with Christinia and other women they were familiar with and the Holy Spirit of course. We used all sorts of methods and teaching, and everyone began to contribute to the activities. It was messy and disruptive, and I wondered if I had the skills to do this. On my last Sunday we visited the prison with Christinia and her Russian team who played music and sang. I chose to do a piece about mother and child. The women could paint or draw either themselves with their mother or their child. This brought up many emotions, cries from the heart for children they were unable to see or mothers who had died. It seemed everyone had a story of heartache. Again, the day began to unravel as it had done previously but this time I felt the presence of the Holy Spirit flood the room. Someone began to sing a Russian worship song which spoke to the women in their own language. Everywhere people began to weep and were on their knees. People were asking for prayer for their unborn child or a lost relationship or forgiveness and wanting salvation. It was time for me to just get out of the way and let the Holy Spirit work. It was an amazing day.

To put it simply we do not get what we think we are going to get when we yield to the Holy Spirit and allow God to use us in the way He wants to. God provided everybody I needed to serve Him. I was just the catalyst to answer the prayers for five women who faithfully served by going into the prison every week. When we debriefed after what would become my last class, Christinia said her team had been going into the prison for 10 years, but they had become dry, so for 2 years they prayed for inspiration and to have a bigger team. I learned that previously they had gone in just to minister to the children. To play games with them and do activities. It never occurred to Christinia or the team to minister the mothers and so now they had a whole new way of approaching their ministry and they were very excited, inspired and happy their prayers were answered.

Yielding

God is our Teacher

Yielding is part of intimacy with God, a one-on-one time. God is your teacher, your mentor, your father, your friend. No-one can help you with this yielding stuff: it is all between you and our Father. It is, however, worth pursuing. You may be surprised how easily obedience works. We have a free will and God gives us choices. You might imagine walking into the sea. You just put your toe in the water, and it is most likely cold, but you manage to allow the water up to your ankles. Just allow the water to wash over your feet. Allow Jesus to wash away your sins with the blood of Christ. Allow God to make suggestions in your prayers. You are not risking very much by responding – in fact it is quite a low level of risk and so there is nothing to lose but there is so much to be gained. Once you are used to the temperature of the water washing over your feet, go a little deeper and see how good it feels. The deeper you go the more confident you become, the more He expresses His love to you, making you feel like you are the only person in the world. Your level of trust grows, eventually to the point where you want to be fully immersed in the water, wanting to be with him always. And He wants to be with you too.

Questions

What if I want to do it my own way?

You do not have to yield to God, but His response is simple. He will use someone else in your place and your dreams will slip away letting down those around you. It sounds harsh but that was my experience. God asked me to do something, and I chose not to do it because I did not think I was hearing God correctly. It was a big lesson for me. The enemy does not want you to win this struggle. He will try with all its might to stop you from yielding. Giving you messages of common sense and logic and not spiritual discernment. We need to step apart from the world by giving up control, accepting the will of God. Thankful He chose us to be His salt and light in a world of darkness. Keep your eyes focused on Jesus while you wrestle in giving things over to Him. You will find that there are things that he wants to give you. He gives far more than He asks for. It is a remarkable feeling: you are with Him and He opens doors, and we simply step through. He makes it easy for us, so allow Him.

What if you have tried in the past to yield to God but you failed?

It is possible your expectations are too high. God asks us to do small things, to take little steps. Those little steps become part of a bigger picture. You could be trying too hard or trying to change something that God does not want changed. He loves you the way you are, even the

Yielding

bits you do not like, that you think should be changed. This is a lesson I need to remember myself. God keeps using me the way I am, not the way I think I should be! Sometimes we need to change our expectations because yielding to God's power means things may not go the way we think they should go. Stay in the present, do not be in the future or the past. He wants you right here, right now – this is your time. Stay focused 100% on doing what it is He has put in front of you, because if you look at where you are going, it is too frightening. You become afraid and overwhelmed.

What if I forget to be obedient?

It is super hard to be obedient all the time. It is a lifelong journey, a marathon not a sprint. There are examples in the Bible of people struggling with God over all sorts of things. Do not expect to get it right first go or second or third for that matter. You just need to take one step at a time. Keep putting God first in all you do. Eventually, you will look back and see where you were and where you are now. You may not be the same person. God has made you the person He called you to be.

Action Plan

Try travelling to a new location, either the mountains, the sea or anywhere in between, because it often helps with receiving new experiences. Through reading Moses' story, we know how much he struggled. He did not start by giving the people the Ten Commandments with a confident voice. He was a humble shepherd for a long time getting to know God, building up a relationship of trust and commitment.

STEP 9

RESTING

Having done all the hard work and being almost ready to begin your new adventure, it is important to rest, because you have been busy preparing, juggling work and ministry commitments. We find this promise in Hebrews 4:9-11 NIV: 'There remains, then, a sabbath-rest for the people of God; for anyone who enters God's rest also rests from their works, just as God did from His.' God created the sabbath to rest because it is beneficial. Being in God's presence, enjoying His word, singing His praises and praying restores us. It is time to rest in Christ. If you arrive exhausted everything will be a struggle. In the months to come there are many things to learn, so it is good to be your best self. To be fresh is a good start.

Take wisdom from those who've gone before. Statistically 12,000 missionaries leave the field each year – 50% leave the field in the first year for preventable reasons.[14] Some of the reasons people leave the field are conflict, fatigue and exhaustion. It is vital for your mental health to rest. God has moulded and prepared you for the many changes to come. You have learned new things in your journey so far. A rest will improve your concentration and memory. It will also reduce levels of stress and even improve your mood. Being in the best possible condition both physically and emotionally when you arrive helps prevent burnout. By fully resting it allows your body's inner healing to activate. It repairs itself and recovers. We all have expectations of being able to do more than is physically possible. Learning to put boundaries in place helps prevent fatigue.

Excitement is building now. You have completed all the tasks of finding an agency, building a prayer team and raising support. Do not hurry onto the plane but enjoy the moment. This is the last time you will be in your home culture, speaking your own language and eating your own food for some time. Make memories that will sustain you through the tough times of being homesick. One of the common reasons missionaries leave the field early is because they become homesick. You will not return home the same person as you left, so savour the moments with family and friends before you depart. They too need to have good memories of your laughter and love for them.

Resting

Having spent many hours in prayer and fasting as the Lord has been teaching you, take a break from internal, external, moral and spiritual struggles. You have learned to hear His voice, learned to listen and learned to yield. It is time to chill. He has moulded you for His purpose and strengthened you with His love. Now is the time to let Him do His thing. Let Him go before you and prepare the way. It is time to take a break from all human effort. Allow God to be God. Trust in His promises for your future. Put your faith in His word that He will provide all you need.

On arrival you are going to be met by new people who will be very excited to greet you. Hospitality is a big thing in many countries. They have been preparing for your arrival for a long time and they will want immediate attention to show you everything about their country, their culture and their food. It is all new to you and the changes are both stimulating and exhausting. The locals will show you the way things are done and want to know the way you do things. They will have many questions. It is a steep learning curve ahead.

This is the beginning of a different type of lifestyle. You are now being financially supported by others. Most of us are fiercely independent so it is quite an adjustment to feel we are being kept by people we may not even know. People work hard in their jobs every day and they are paying for you to be a missionary. You will feel the need to get onto the field straight away to do stuff. You are no longer earning your own income. You are reliant on the generosity of others. This brings up a whole new set of emotions. You might think how can I justify my time? Who am I answerable to? I must work harder. Do not feel guilty for taking time to slow down and take time out for yourself. No-one is expecting a superhuman effort. People understand missionaries get tired just like everyone else. The enemy uses guilt to prevent us from God's work. Do not allow him the opportunity to enter your world.

Resting in God means to release our burdens for Jesus to carry them. Rest is trust. Rest means quieting our thoughts, worries and concerns by turning them over to God. Rest gives us peace of mind and soul. Resting in God at the end of your preparation time also means He will support you. He has your back. You know that you are in safe hands and being well cared for. He has prepared you for the coming adventure. He has been moulding you and you have been yielding to Him. Now this is the beginning of a new story with Him. Now you are going to be His hands and His feet. Now you are going to share the gospel with the lost and help the poor with their needs.

Carl Strehlow Hermannsburg (1871–1922) was a linguist and anthropologist. He established the much-loved Hermannsburg Mission for the Aboriginal community in the Northern Territory in 1877.[15]

Patience

For some people going onto the field is a real challenge. Stopping and listening to what God wants you to do next is difficult. Learning to be patient is hard for all of us.

I liken it to building a house. When we begin building a new house we are faced with an enormous task. We have a vision and ideas of what it might look like. We get money for the project and engage an architect. The architect works with us to create a plan to fit the vision. The plans need to be approved which always takes longer than we imagine. There is often much anguish in the details between the architect and the planning committee as both try to close the gulf between the wants and the needs of all the interested parties. Along comes the builder. He relies on reading the plans. He does not have a vision or the same urgency you have for getting the house finished. It is simply another job for them. It is possible to make the mistake of moving into the house before the work is complete. Everything is almost done, and you desperately want to move in now. You are so excited, having waited so long that you just need to do it immediately and those little jobs that you didn't do or didn't get done sometimes they never get done and you look back and think, why was I so impatient? It would only take just a little longer to finish everything well.

Finishing well is satisfying and pleasing to God. Calmness, grace and dignity is in keeping with our faith. Leaving this way gives a lasting impression of inspiration on those we are leaving behind and those who may be inspired to follow in our footsteps.

Departure time

It is emotional saying goodbye to those you love, so don't rush it. You want to give yourself the best possible chance to have a fruitful ministry. Thinking of how others are feeling at this point doesn't come naturally. We are all wound up in excitement and fear and the last thing that comes to mind is how others might be feeling.

I liken the departure of missionaries to this. Some plants lie dormant in the winter. A plant may look dead with nothing much happening, but it has been very busy. It starts to germinate and grow as it comes into spring. There are new shoots starting to emerge. With fruit trees when the weather is warmer, we see the fruit appear after being dormant so long. This adventure is coming to life, and you need to relish the moment. New plants have a wonderful way of bringing light and life into the world.

The world you are stepping into is full of spiritual darkness and you are bringing Jesus' light and life into it. But you are not an island. You have only arrived at this point through the work of many who have helped you to get this far. Parents, teachers, friends, work colleagues, counsellors, youth leaders and so on. Share this moment with them. Celebrate by saying goodbye well. Allowing them to share in your joy and excitement fills our hearts to overflowing. People care about you and want the best for you. They

Resting

have watched you blossom over many years. Cherish this moment.

God gives a wonderful picture for us to leave with. Reading Psalms is comforting. We receive messages and pictures that help us where we are at. Psalm 23:5-6, NIV: 'You prepare a table before me in the presence of my enemies. You anoint my head with oil, my cup overflows. Surely your goodness and love will follow me all the days of my life, and I will dwell in the house of the Lord forever.'

God uses the picture of a table with you as His honoured guest and He has prepared a banquet for you. He is telling you He will sustain you by strengthening you. Your body is given strength through a good meal and God will feed you to sustain you. Nothing will separate you from His unfailing love.

We may experience trials, but they only help us grow closer to God and more dependent on Him. God anoints your head as a sign you are set apart for His divine purposes and protection.

Questions

What if I have no time to rest before I leave?

You are the one in control of your own destiny. You are in charge of when you leave for the field. If you decide you need to rest, I am sure people will respect that decision.

We spend our whole lives rushing around to get to this meeting or that event but there comes a time when enough is enough and we must stop.

What if I can't say goodbye?

To some people this question may sound silly, but my mother was someone who never said goodbye. It was always too traumatic, and she never knew what to say. I think of it as a gift to those I love. It's not about me, it's about the ones I'm saying goodbye to. No-one likes to say goodbye, but if you can develop the skill it's going to be very handy on the field because you are always saying goodbye.

What if I'm not ready to leave?

An agency will give you a checklist to make sure you have thought of everything you need. No-one is ever ready to leave. There is always more to learn, more to prepare for. It's like stepping into the unknown and that can be frightening

Resting

Action Plan

I believe it's important to stop on the way to your location. Find somewhere in the world that's warm and comfortable like Thailand. Many missionaries use Thailand as a place to rest. The Thai people are kind and humble with servant hearts. In Thailand there are several Christian mission retreat places, so it is inexpensive. I suggest stopping there for about 2 weeks to gather yourself. To be alone with God. Use the wisdom of those who have gone before you and take a break. Arriving stressed and tired is not the impression you want to give. When there's no-one else around, just you and God hanging out together it is rewarding. Enjoy going for a walk, eating well, strengthening your body, having someone take care of your every need. Being emotionally and physically prepared you can expect things will go well. It is not taking a holiday, it is rest and recovery. I think this is a good practice for agencies to embrace so the new missionary has a good outcome in their first few months, so they do not suffer burnout or get homesick or fight with their teammates.

STEP 10

FAQ

Where should I go?

A very good question. Sometimes it's just taking hold of opportunities that are before you. Your church may be doing a short-term mission trip somewhere and you could go and explore what the longer-term possibilities are. Or better still to discern what God is saying to you.

You may have always had a heart or a burden for a particular place or people group. Take it that this is from God. So, explore what mission agencies are operating in those countries or to those people groups. Get on their mailing list and start praying for those works and even financially supporting them.

If your heart is truly for mission to some area it is likely that you are already supporting them in some way. Keep praying for God to lead you and for Him to open the right doors. If there is a door before you, give it a bit of a push and see if it opens for you.

God's promise to you is that as you submit your ways and desires to Him, He will lead you. So, as in everything, keep close to God and He will bring about His plans and purposes for you.

When you believe God is showing you the direction then take at least small steps in that direction. Sometimes we are waiting for God when He's really waiting for us to respond to what He has already shown us.

What should I do to prepare myself?

So, you feel the call to be a missionary or at least to go to the mission field. How can you prepare yourself?

The first is spiritually. Make sure you have put God first in all areas of your life. Pray for God to show you if there are any areas which are unyielded to Him.

Prepare what you think God wants you to do. Maybe get involved with similar things at home. There is a saying that

FAQ

you can't be a missionary overseas if you are not one at home first. Learn what is available in those areas of ministry.

A big part of any ministry must be taking up the opportunities to share the gospel. Practise sharing the gospel with friends and others at home. Even practise with your church in small groups. Better still get involved with an evangelism training and practical group at home, for example, Australia for Jesus. This will give you tools and confidence to share your faith. Practise sharing your testimony too.

Maybe you can do some Bible studies. Bible colleges have courses that equip you for missions. They cover a range of relevant practical topics that will prepare you well. They will connect you with other people who have a similar calling and with mission agencies and other organisations that can help you prepare. You are not alone, and you are not meant to prepare alone, so connect with other people and groups that are promoting missions and preparing people for answering His call.

Involve yourself with mission agencies at home. They often have courses and training to help prepare you for your future endeavours. These are practical and equip you well for all the uncertain situations you will face as you go onto the mission field.

What should I do in the mission field?

What are your gifts? What have you been involved with at home? What do you do in the church and outside the church? These should give you clues as to your capabilities and calling. Are you a people person or an administrator? Are you a teacher or pastoral?

Your role on the mission field will likely have some relationship to your role at home. What are the needs that you think you can help meet? What are the roles being sought by the mission agency that seem to fit your liking and abilities?

The answer to these questions should help you commit to a particular role that is being sought on the field.

Being flexible is very much part of a missionary's call. There will be needs and opportunities on the field that you feel called to contribute to. Don't be so fixed in your role that you can't do other things as the opportunity arises. You might be amazed at what you can do and can be part of as you step into new areas that God is calling you to be part of.

What if the money I need is not coming in?

Be assured, this is not an unusual situation. God is often using this season of support raising to teach you to trust in Him and that He will provide. But it is a testing time

FAQ

too, so keep looking to God, asking Him to guide you. And trust Him.

Be open to the different things He is saying to you, and even through other people and your mission agency. You may learn to try different approaches, do uncomfortable things and go where you are not intending. Even asking family members if they will support you.

Talk to others about their experiences. Many have stories of the trials of support raising but then the joys of seeing God provide. He has called you. He will get you there. Keep trusting and keep moving forward.

Be open to the possibility of tent making. This can have many advantages, not just for the provision of finance. Sometimes work will help with an entry visa, or connections with non-believers in a country. Remember what God has called you to and don't allow work to be your main purpose. These days many companies are open to part-time employment.

How do I prepare for culture shock?

Can you prepare for culture shock? If you do it won't shock you. There will always be things you don't expect. If you have travelled before, especially to Third World countries you will be better prepared for things that are different. If not you can always read, listen to podcasts or watch documentaries that will help you understand the culture you are going into. There is information on different cultures, hot and cold countries and other people's world view.

Expect that some things will be strange and different and may shock you. Accept these differences as not necessarily being wrong (although some may be) and very much part of the norm for the people you will be ministering to. Your journey onto the mission field will be a learning path for you. As you build relationships with people you will find that we have much more in common. We all value people and families. Be accepting and you will find the process of culture learning a very rewarding one.

However, be aware that this process will also take its toll. You may be burdened or tired or even depressed and angry as you continually try and deal with different situations. Do give yourself a break at times. Connect with people of your own culture, and plan to take a holiday each year to step aside from the work and the culture learning, so you can go back enthusiastic to keep learning and keep connecting with the people God has called you to.

Is it right to leave your family?

This somewhat depends on the age of your kids, the needs of your parents, and how you view those responsibilities. If God has called you, He will provide, not just for you but for them as well.

FAQ

It is all about obeying God and trusting God. Interestingly, when Geoff and I returned from serving overseas (even though it was due to Covid), it was a new calling to look after and be with family, both parents in need as well as children who were having their own children. God's timing was perfect and so you can trust Him also to look after all that concerns you and to work out all things in accordance with his plans and purposes (Rom 8:28 NIV).

What if I'm no good at learning language?

Someone once told me, of course you can learn language. You have already learnt one! However, I don't think that is a fair comment. Let's face it, some people are good at learning languages, and some are not.

My experience with struggling with learning language was to keep trying. Concentrating on the essentials of basic customary cultural greetings, along with simple language like saying hello, goodbyes, thank you and pleases, as well as smaller talk about family and children and even weather was all helpful. People will usually respect you if you are trying because it means you respect them. Often a person will have some basic English, and they want to practise that on you too. This will build relationships with people despite your bad language learning if you keep trying to improve. Your friends you are acquiring will often feel special being able to teach you.

Bad language will frustrate some, especially those you are dealing with in government agencies such as immigration and any permit issuer. So it is good to have a local friend to accompany you in those situations, to be your translator.

Limited language will have its limitations for your relationship with people. You might connect well to talk about family and work and weather, but to go deeper to discuss the deeper things of life and faith will be difficult. By using locals to share the gospel, we are replacing ourselves.

But don't despair. While you are continuing to learn language, you are growing those relationships that might eventually lead to deep ministry connections, or these people might be your eternal joy and crown (Phil 4:1 NIV).

What agency should I go with?

Most people go with an agency they know or have been introduced too. Think about the country and the people group you believe God is calling you to. Research the different agencies that go to that country and the type of work done. Does that fit your profile?

Talk to others who are associated with the agency or read their website, newsletters or blogs. It's an important decision, and there is no need to decide quickly. Give God time to move you into the place he wants you to serve.

FAQ

How long should I plan to go for?

This is very dependent on a lot of factors. People leave the field when their children need to go to secondary school in their home country. Some stay till old age long after their original term of commitment. Some just go for a 5 or 10-year assignment then return regularly. Everybody's situation will be different.

Some sending churches have a policy of limiting the term with a requirement for you to go with an exit strategy, like how long it will take to train up locals and hand over the work to them.

Your mission organisation will likely have a lot to say about the term of your engagement that fits with their bigger picture of the work they are doing in that country.

Generally, you will return home at regular intervals. At certain times you will have to reassess your direction and commitment and even raise more support for the next season. That can affect how long you go for. Age and health are also factors that have a strong influence on your term.

Bottom line: go with a plan but be open and flexible to change that plan to suit changing needs and circumstances. Always be open to God's leading and direction.

What academic qualifications do I need?

Academic qualifications are not normally required to be a missionary, but some agencies require formal qualifications. They may be needed for some roles such as starting or being part of a Bible training college. Qualifications may help you get a visa and gain access to certain countries. You might go as a teacher for example and so will need formal teacher qualifications.

Formal qualifications are not generally necessary but may be advantageous. You might do a Bible college course to prepare yourself for going. You might have formal accounting or managerial qualifications that have equipped you for administration or other work at home and that will equip you for similar roles on the field.

Don't let a lack of formal qualifications deter you from applying and obeying God's call to go. Show the mission agency that you have gifts and abilities by putting together a detailed CV outlining what you have been involved with, both with work and in the church. They will also be looking to ascertain your gifts and abilities so don't be backward in outlining what your strengths are. These have been given by God for you to use in your mission calling.

What if the country is not 100% safe?

No country is 100% safe. We can get run over by a bus at home or persecuted by family members being against us.

FAQ

However, some countries are less safe than others. I would recommend following Australian Government travel recommendations. If they say don't travel there then I would be getting out, at least until the situation improves.

Ultimately, we are following God. God calls some to go to high-risk countries, but you must know absolutely that God is calling you there. The normal ways of discerning God's will apply, and then checking with Godly counsel such as your local church leadership or missions committee or some people you trust.

There are risks in any country and it is good to assess these risks, which your mission organisation has probably already done. They want to see you safe as much as you do. But there are always risks of things happening or things changing in the country where you go to serve.

Having a contingency plan and an exit strategy is a must. How will you get out if an emergency happens? Be sensible, not a martyr. What are you doing compared to other missionaries in that country or in other similar countries? Do some homework so you are well informed to make wise decisions.

Listen to what is God is saying to you in prayer and keep close connections with your home church and your missionary organisation people at home.

Consider the possibility of dying or getting seriously injured on the field. Again, have a plan for this. Take out insurances and have a will. Being cremated is usual for most insurance plans. Most agencies will discuss this with you. A plan will make it easier for you and for your family at home. They care about you too.

How do I know this is God?

We start with the Word of God. We learn lessons from Jesus because through Him we will learn about the Father because they are one and the same. Fathers love to talk to their children and the Lord is no different. He wants a relationship with you.

Reading scripture regularly teaches, encourages and corrects us.

Make a commitment to follow Jesus no matter what the cost.

He will make a commitment to you too. He may come to you in dreams and in visions. He may send an angel or a godly person with wisdom and discernment. He may show you things through circumstances and events. He will suggest ideas in your mind and give you passion in your heart.

He loves you no matter what.

AFTERWORD

WORD.

We know and understand Jesus through reading the Bible. Jesus pours out His love for us every day. His love is forgiving for those who come to him and repent and believe in eternal life. His Word is our guide, our teacher and comforter. Through the Word, God is present with us. He is the light that shines through the darkness.

Psalm 119:105 NIV: 'The Word is a lamp unto my feet and a light unto my path.'

PURPOSE.

We desire to know what our purpose for life is. This is a common theme throughout the history of mankind. To leave something behind for the benefit of others or the planet. This sense of calling leads many to serve Him on the mission field. As we discover more about Christ we discover more about our identity and purpose. We are empowered by the Holy Spirit who gives us vision and direction.

Ecclesiastes 3:12-13 NIV: 'I know that there is nothing better for people than to be happy and to do good while they live. That each of them may eat and drink and find satisfaction in all their toil – this is a gift from God.'

DEVOTION.

Our time spent in devotion brings us closer to our Father. As we chew over His words in our mind they seep into our hearts. He reveals many things to us. He moulds us as we yield to Him. The more we pray the more He shows himself to us. The more we trust Him the more He trusts us.

Romans 12:9-12 NIV: 'Love must be sincere. Hate what is evil; cling to what is good. Be devoted to one another in love. Honour one another above ourselves. Never be lacking in zeal, but keep your spiritual fervour, serving the Lord.'

SALVATION.

Jesus shows us the way to the Father through the New Testament. We can believe in the Lord because He never changes, He is present, and He is trustworthy. Salvation is personal but we long to share it with others to open their eyes to His love for us all for now and eternity. He answers our questions, who am I and why am I here? The journey of salvation brings us to a place of awakening to save us from sin that separates us from Him.

Afterword

Romans 8:28-30 NIV: 'And we know that in all things God works for the good of those who love Him, who have been called according to His purpose. For those God foreknew he also predestined to be conformed to the image of His son that He might be the first born among many brothers and sisters. And those he predestined He also called; those He called He also justified; those He justified He also glorified.'

This, then, is how you should pray:

Our Father in heaven, hallowed be your name. Your kingdom come; your will be done on earth as in heaven. Give us today our daily bread. And forgive us our sins, lead us not into temptation, but deliver us from evil. (Matt 6:9-13 NIV)

ABOUT THE AUTHOR

Amanda lives in the picturesque Adelaide Hills with her husband and a few sheep. In her youth she trained as a chef at Le Cordon Bleu in Paris and lived with a French family as an au pair. She travelled and worked throughout Europe before opening her own seafood restaurant with her husband in Port Fairy in southwest Victoria, Australia. Following the birth of her two sons she moved to South Australia where she qualified as an investment adviser. Amanda worked with women to help them learn about finances. After her husband passed away in her early fifties, she returned to university to complete a Bachelor of Theology and met her second husband. Together, with his youngest son, they embarked on an adventure living and working in Central Asia as missionaries and then in Latvia. She worked with trafficked and imprisoned women. Amanda is now mentoring other women to live and work as long-term missionaries. It is her passion to see people well prepared to work on the field to be part of the global harvest.

REFERENCES

Step 1: Calling

[1] Royal Flying Doctor Service, *John Flynn Biography*, https://www.flyingdoctor.org.au/about-the-rfds/history/john-flynn-bio/

Step 2: Positioning

[2] Tony Cupit, Ros Gooden and Ken Manley, *From Five Barley Loaves: Australian Baptists in Global Mission*, (Morning Star, 2011), https://www.baptistmissionaustralia.org

[3] Suzanne Pearson, 'Missions vocabulary 101': Common Missionary lingo Easily Defined. Team -The Evangelical, Mission Life, https://www.team.org/article/missions-vocabulary-101/

Step: 3 Fear

[4] Ruth Lee (ed), *The Encyclopedia of Women & Leadership in Twentieth Century Australia*, (Australian Women's Archives Project, 2014), https://www.womenaustralia.info/leaders/about.html

Step 4: Agencies

[5] Alan Tippett. *Alan R. Tippett Series*, (William Carey Publishing) https://missionbooks.org/collections/alan-r-tippett-series

Step 5: Praying

[6] Eugene Peterson, *Eat this Book*, (Hachette Book Group, 2008).

[7] Tony Glynn Southern Cross University. *Celebrating 20 years of the Father*, published August 2024, University News. https://www.scu.edu.au/news/2024/celebrating-20-years-of-the-father-tony-glynn-japan-australia-centre/

Step 6: Moulding

[8] Sophia Blackmore: National Library Board. Singapore Infopedia https://www.nlb.gov.sg/main/article-detail?cmsuuid=a740ec0f-8d09-40c0-b5e9-43f6dbf6c2c4

References

Step 7: Fundraising

[9] Tony de Bolfo, *Brook Hannah: God's Footballer*, published August 2014 https://www.carltonfc.com.au/news/713709/gods-footballer

[10] Betty Barnett, *Building a Missionary Support Team that Lasts*, (YWAM, 2002 rev ed.)

Step 8: Yielding

[11] Sarah J Hauser, *Find Freedom from Self Condemnation*, (The Gospel Coalition, 2023), https://www.thegospelcoalition.org/article/freedom-self-condemnation/

[12] Paul Akin, *The Number One Reason Missionaries Leave the Field*, (Baptist Press, 2017), https://www.baptistpress.com/resource-library/news/the-number-one-reason-missionaries-leave-the-field/

[13] Fred and Betty Evans website, https://www.fredandbettyevans.com/

Step 9: Resting

[14] 2024 Christian Missionary Statistics. Nations Outreach. By Jeremy Koeing March 1, 2024.
https://nationsoutreach.org/stories/christian-missionary-statistics/

[15] National Heritage Places. Hermannsburg Historical Precinct - DCCEEW
https://www.dcceew.gov.au/parks-heritage/heritage/places/national/hermannsburg

EXPLANATION OF THE SYMBOLS

Step 1

Alpha is the first letter of the Greek alphabet and Omega is the last. Together these two letters form a monogram or symbol for one of the names of Jesus Christ, meaning 'the Beginning and the End'. The term is found in Revelation 1:8: 'I am the Alpha and the Omega,' says the Lord God, 'who is, and who was, and who is to come, the Almighty.' (NIV) Two more times in the book of Revelation we see this name for Jesus.

Step 2

The Cross and Crown is a familiar symbol in Christian churches. It represents the reward awaiting in heaven (the crown) that believers will receive after the suffering and trials of life on earth (the cross).

Step 3

The Lamb of God represents Jesus Christ, the perfect, sinless sacrifice offered by God to atone for the sins of man.

Step 4

The dove represents the Holy Spirit, or Holy Ghost, in Christianity. The Holy Spirit descended upon Jesus like a dove when He was baptised in the Jordan River.

Step 5

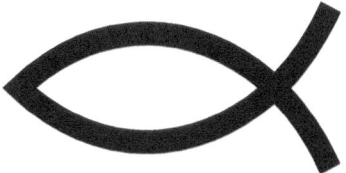

The Christian Fish, also called the Jesus Fish or Ichthys, was a secret symbol of early Christianity.

Step 6

The Triquetra is an ancient pagan symbol found on Celtic period grave markers that is used to represent a three-part interlocking fish symbol for the Christian Trinity.

Step 7

The Star of David is a six-pointed star formed by two interlocking triangles, one pointing up, one pointing down. It is named after King David and appears on the flag of Israel. While predominantly recognised as a symbol of Judaism and Israel, many Christians identify with the Star of David as well.

Step 8

This is the ancient monogram for Jesus that dates back to the first century. It is an abbreviation derived from the first three letters (iota=i+eta=h+sigma=s) of the Greek word 'Jesus'. Scribes wrote a line or bar over the letters to indicate an abbreviation.

Step 9

Chi-Rho is the oldest known monogram (or letter symbol) for Christ. Some call this symbol the 'Christogram' and it dates back to the Roman Emperor Constantine (A.D. 306-337).

Step 10

With so many references to God being 'light' in Scripture, representations of light such as candles, flames and lamps have become common symbols of Christianity.

ACKNOWLEDGEMENTS

This book is dedicated to my parents, Wilma and Austin Lewis. My father continually encouraged me to strive to be the best I could be. He would be delighted to know I have written a book. Unfortunately, he passed away last year. He instilled in me the importance of family and relationships, and to set goals and work towards achieving them.

Many thanks to my husband Geoff, who like my father, encouraged me and supported me to reach my goals on many different occasions. Even to the point of living on frozen meals for a month while I focused on my writing. Thanks also to my wonderful children for their interest and encouragement during the process.

I would like to thank all those who have contributed to helping this book to come to completion. There were many things I learned along the way. Thanks to Natasa and Stuart Denman and the staff at Ultimate 48 Hour Author for their unfailing dedication, enthusiasm and commitment to helping me share my insights with others. Thanks to Marinda Wilkinson for her patience and excellent editing skills which allowed my voice to be heard. Thanks to Nikola Boskovski for his cover design and easy-going manner. Nothing was too much trouble.

To all those missionaries I have met on my journey and have gathered inspiration and information from, I pray they continue to seek and serve the Lord in all they do. Lastly, I am eternally grateful to God for His guidance giving me an understanding of who I am, and the role I play in serving Him.

CONTACT AMANDA

If you would like to discuss speaking opportunities at your conference, mission organisation event, or would like some questions answered, please get in touch. Today's technology allows us to interact easily.

By phone: 0466333222 (please leave a message)
By email: Amanda@answering-his-call.com
By mail: PO Box 18 Stirling 5152 South Australia

Or follow on social media:
Facebook: Amanda Dyer Author
Instagram: Answering_His_Call
Website: answering-his-call.com

We all have challenges in our mission journey. Something may have blocked your path, and you are unable to see the way forward. It might be a hidden belief, a fear, or a regretted missed opportunity. Engaging with someone with a fresh pair of eyes may help get you back on track.

Amanda may be engaged to provide mentoring services (by negotiation).

FREE WORKBOOK AVAILABLE ONLINE

To help you apply the learnings of this book, Amanda has made available a free downloadable workbook that gives you questions to answer for each step in your calling adventure.

Please scan this QR code and then subscribe to receive this workbook.

NOTES

Answering HIS Call

Notes

www.ingramcontent.com/pod-product-compliance
Lightning Source LLC
Chambersburg PA
CBHW030324080526
44584CB00012B/701